NORTH SEA PORTRAITS

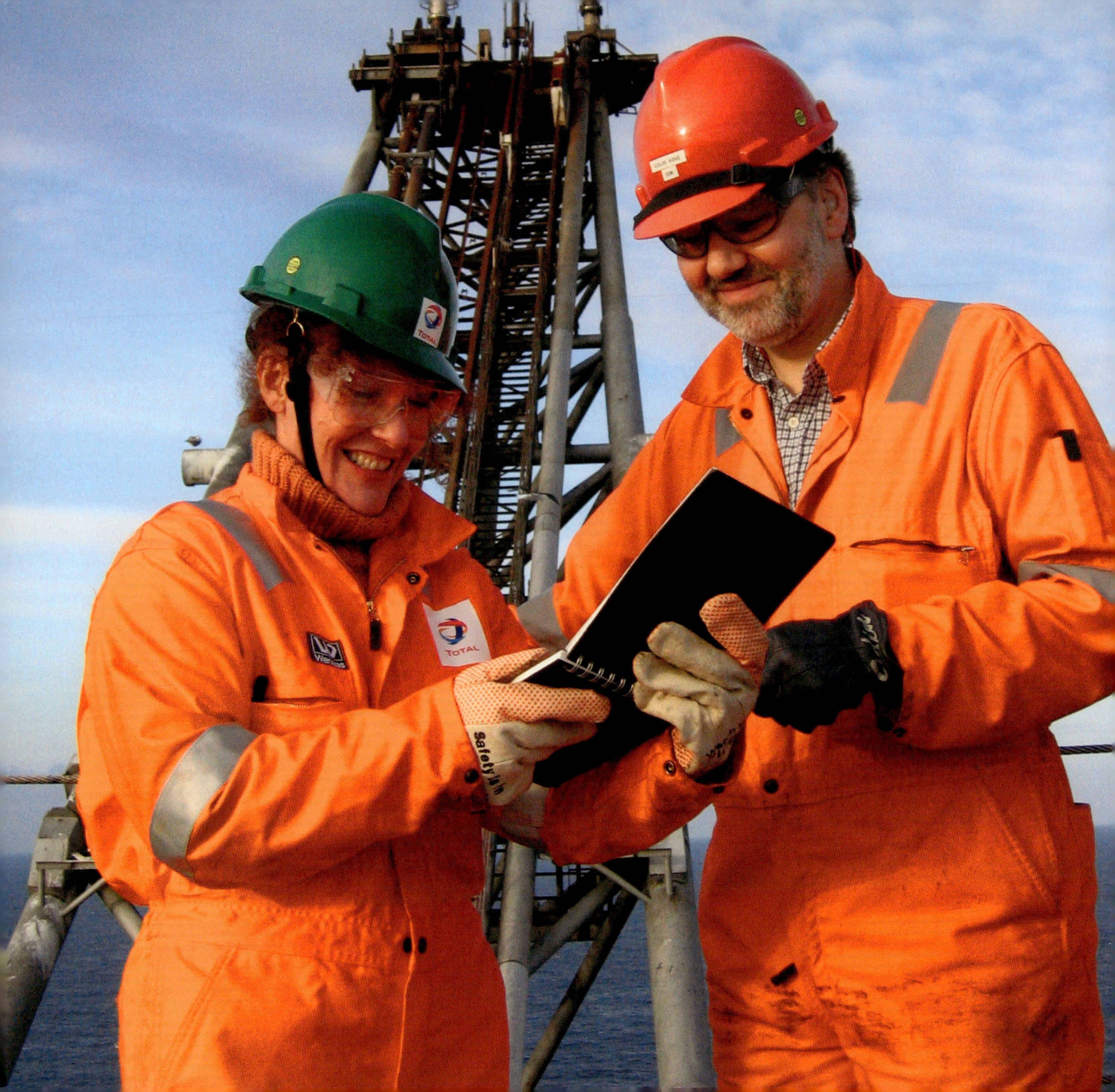
TOTAL

ENERGY

North Sea Portraits · Fionna Carlisle

NATIONAL GALLERIES OF SCOTLAND · 2006

Foreword

The Scottish National Portrait Gallery is an institution that aims to record and affirm the diversity and achievement of Scots from all walks of life, past and present. As such, its collection, exhibitions and publications form a unique visual record of a changing country and society.

It is often through collaboration that this has been achieved. The project *Energy: North Sea Portraits* has been realised thanks to Total – a particularly fortunate and fruitful collaboration for us. Working closely with Total, and the distinguished artist Fionna Carlisle, we have been able to mount this exhibition of portraits of individuals representing the astounding variety of tasks necessary for the successful operation of the North Sea oil industry. There are portraits of geologists, rig-builders, economists, helicopter pilots, the technical and service staff on the rigs themselves, and others – all of whom have been chosen to represent the many aspects of this vital industry.

Total, supported by an Arts & Business New Partners Investment, has very generously funded and played host to the artist, Fionna Carlisle. She has been enabled to explore the industry – at sea, on shore and airborne – and depict, thanks to her own daring and skill, these ingenious, enterprising and intrepid individuals.

The National Galleries of Scotland is delighted by the outcome of this collaboration with Total and Fionna Carlisle. This project has also been undertaken in partnership with Aberdeen Maritime Museum, where the portraits will be shown after their exhibition in Edinburgh, and with Highland Council who will feature the work prominently in 2007, the Year of Highland Culture.

At the end of the tour, four of the portraits will be given to the collection of the Scottish National Portrait Gallery, where they will play an important part in telling the story of modern Scotland.

JOHN LEIGHTON
Director-General, National Galleries of Scotland

JAMES HOLLOWAY
Director, Scottish National Portrait Gallery

Sponsor's Foreword

Life on the oil rigs is often seen as remote, but there is a vibrant community of people working throughout the sector, providing an incredible range of skills – both at sea and on land. *Energy: North Sea Portraits* aims to capture all levels of the industry at a critical moment in its history. This is one of the most important industries in the country, and one which has revolutionised the United Kingdom's economy. Oil was first pumped ashore thirty years ago and, although volumes being produced are beginning to diminish, on current estimates there remain thirty years' worth of oil reserves still to be claimed from the sea.

Total E&P UK PLC, present in the UK North Sea since 1964, continues to plapjan important role in this achievement. With headquarters in Paris and activities spanning some 130 countries around the world, Total is the fourth largest operator in the UK in terms of production and reserves. From its base in Aberdeen the company operates the fields of the Alwyn Area, which in 2007 celebrates its twentieth year, as well as the high pressure / high temperature Elgin-Franklin field and the St Fergus Gas Terminal. Total takes very seriously its role in the communities in which it operates. Support is given to a wide spectrum of organisations including education, the environment, health and of course the arts. The emphasis is on establishing partnerships within the community and involving staff in local projects.

With this in mind, Total – together with the National Galleries of Scotland and supported by an Arts & Business New Partners Investment – is delighted to support the commission of Fionna Carlisle, one of Scotland's best-known portrait painters, to create these striking works. It is a fitting celebration of the lives and achievement of the people who make up Scotland's oil and gas industry, now and for the future.

ROLAND FESTOR
Managing Director, TOTAL E&P UK PLC

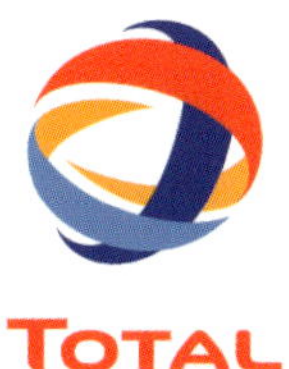

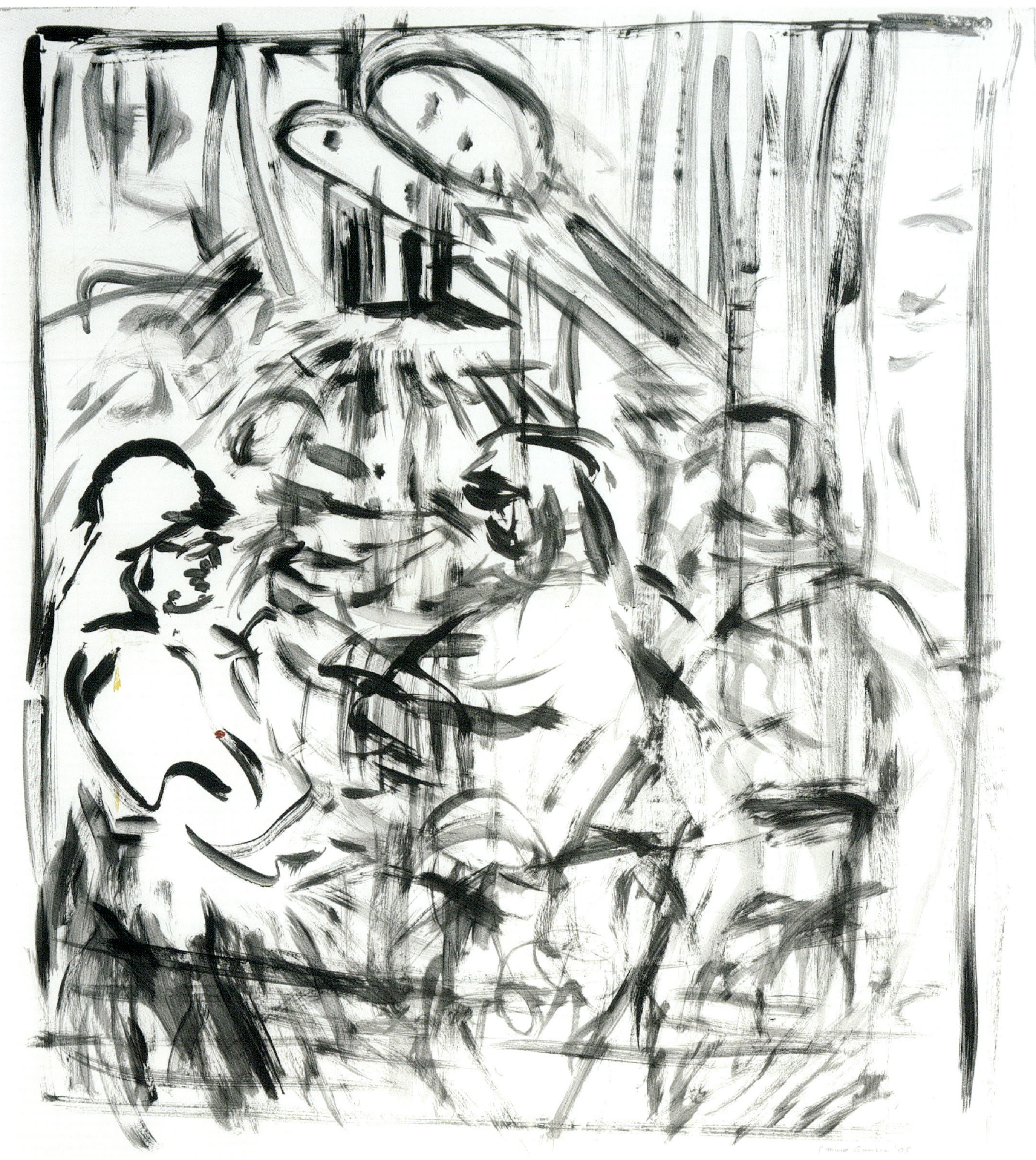

North Sea Pioneers

BILL MACKIE

Drillfloor from doghouse, Alwyn North, 2005
Painted in Xania, Greece · acrylic on paper, 110 x 98

The North Sea oil and gas industry is the great industrial triumph of the twentieth century and the largest, most successful, single enterprise in the modern economic history of Scotland. Massive in concept, in employment, and in the generation of vast wealth, the harvesting of hydrocarbons from some of the most unforgiving waters on Earth has been a triumph of pure human endeavour to equal any achievements in space. The fiscal revenues saved a debt-ridden United Kingdom; vulnerable Scottish communities have been enriched; new opportunities and new companies have emerged; and, from the golden stream of profits, global giants of commerce have grown.

Out of the empty spaces of offshore Britain and in a remarkably brief span of time, thousands of pioneers have created a new world. Bold, brave, imaginative, innovative, and driven by tough, demanding masters they risked their lives and too often, too many died.

The parallel landward invasion round the jagged littorals of east and north-west Scotland and the Northern Isles precipitated an oil rush as thrilling and tumultuous as any nineteenth-century Klondyke; entirely unsolicited, instant modern commerce settled in deprived and stagnating areas, energising the complacent and the comfortable. Designers and builders brought ingenuity and new craftsmanship to revolutionary concepts in concrete and steel, and all on a Herculean scale not seen since the glory days of the Clyde shipyards.

Across the forty-year development of North Sea oil, what happened to Scotland was far beyond the experience of the indigent business and industrial community, but it engendered an extraordinary response from a willing host. Machines found, extracted and developed the oil and gas, but it took an extraordinary breed – the industry's greatest asset – to grow the vibrant new enterprise. Tough, resourceful pioneers, led by hardened veterans of foreign oilfields, operating in a perilous environment and driven ultimately by unimaginable costs – the early drilling crews set the template for what became a multi-national workforce. Many roustabouts and roughnecks fought their way to operational management as production began, and the almost casual meritocracy offshore was reciprocated onshore in the offices, terminals and bases. All this was supported by fearless divers and a motley army manning the daily flocks of helicopters and the tireless supply and standby boats, without whom there would have been no industry.

The heroic saga of the North Sea – for

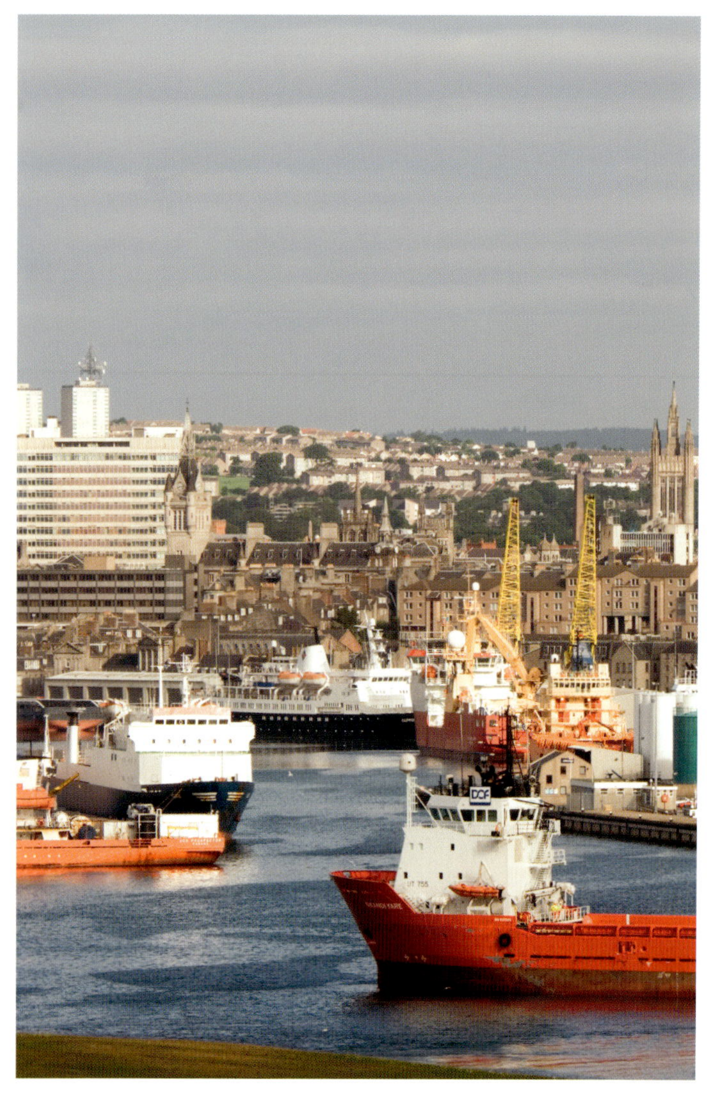

Aberdeen Harbour
Reproduced by kind permission of
Aberdeen Harbour Board

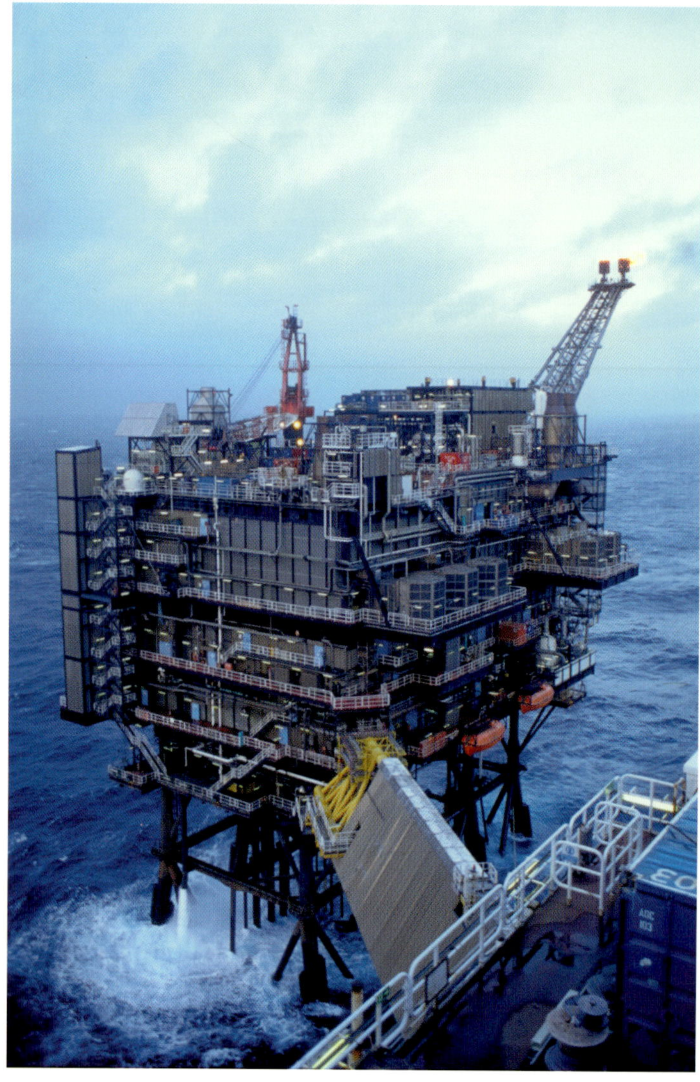

Total's Alwyn North platform

that, undoubtedly, is what it is – began quietly in the mid-1960s, when a small irregular flotilla of frail craft slipped out of the ancient port of Aberdeen, below the north-east shoulder of Scotland, and into the treacherous waters. The crews – geologists and seismologists – sought to prove an academic theory that the seabed harboured secret reservoirs of hydrocarbons, cooked over thousands of years from fossilised deposits in faults and pockets deep within the rock strata. Substantial deposits of commercially viable fossil fuels, in the form of natural gas, had already been found in Holland's northern coastal marshes and in the southern North Sea, but oil men were convinced even greater finds lay out across the 55th parallel.

Subsequently, the first drillers, uncertain what they would encounter, battled northwards in the late 1960s, prospecting 150 miles off Buchan, up into the Moray Firth and to the east of Shetland. Another rig crossed into Norwegian waters, the scene of an earlier small strike. Tormented by the North Sea's notorious gales and towering walls of water, the multi-national consortium led by Phillips, had all but abandoned their search. Then, from the very last hole came an exciting discovery that validated the potential of the northern sector – the giant oil and gas field, Ekofisk.

Natural gas was welcome and came to dominate Britain's domestic energy needs, but the true prize was the more lucrative reservoirs of oil. A BP rig, Sea Quest, was first to find it in the central sector, ironically for the American Oil Consortium (Amoco). Finally at the end of 1969, BP drilled their own treasure trove, the huge and fertile field named after the sea area in which it lay; Forties' oil provided the platform for the world's second biggest energy conglomerate. After a frustrating year of dry holes, Shell's even larger cornucopia, Brent, followed in what became the prolific Shetland basin. Over the next decade more big fields followed for BP, Shell and the other industry leaders, such as Total's huge Frigg gas discovery straddling the international line, their Alwyn Area Field, Mobil's Beryl, Elf's Piper, Conoco's Hutton, Chevron's Ninian. In the following twenty years smaller finds came thick and fast, forging a chain of more than 300 fields from beyond the Northern Isles to the Firth of Forth, and qualifying the UK for the exclusive global club of oil-rich provinces.

The pressure to develop on land was as febrile as at sea. Long before hydrocarbons were found a cluster of companies had established service outposts at Peterhead, Montrose and Dundee, and most importantly, in Aberdeen. Around the east, west and north coastal and island footprint, oil men and construction engineers haggled for space for platform fabrication yards, pipeline and tanker terminals and processing plants.

Around remote, tranquil Highland lochs, across the beaches of peaceful firths, in harbours and over abandoned collieries, vast open workshops proliferated, swarming with thousands of recruits, swiftly burnishing new skills to fashion the stout steel fretwork and concrete carcases of the giants the offshore production force demanded. The massive social incursion was at first feared but ultimately welcomed by communities; weakened by economic neglect and depopulation, they were revived by the flood of employment and new investment the industry brought. Wherever there were bases, and the huge terminals and plants that harvested, processed and pumped out the precious products, there was the same overwhelming impact. Such as on a windy Buchan seashore where a complex of silver pipes and tanks evolved into Europe's biggest gas reception and processing project, Total E&P UK's St Fergus Gas Terminal, supplying twenty per cent of Britain's needs.

As more and more massive production structures emerged from their birthplaces, the wide wastes of the UK continental shelf became populated with virtual marine industrial estates. Inter-linked platforms, embedded with space-age precision, fed the fossil fuels down hundreds of miles of umbilical pipelines, themselves epics of construction. When the first oil from Forties beached in Cruden Bay in 1975, the golden era began. For a time the country achieved self-sufficiency in energy as the wealth stream of billions of pounds flowed into and out of the North Sea in expenditure, profits and in revenues for the British Exchequer.

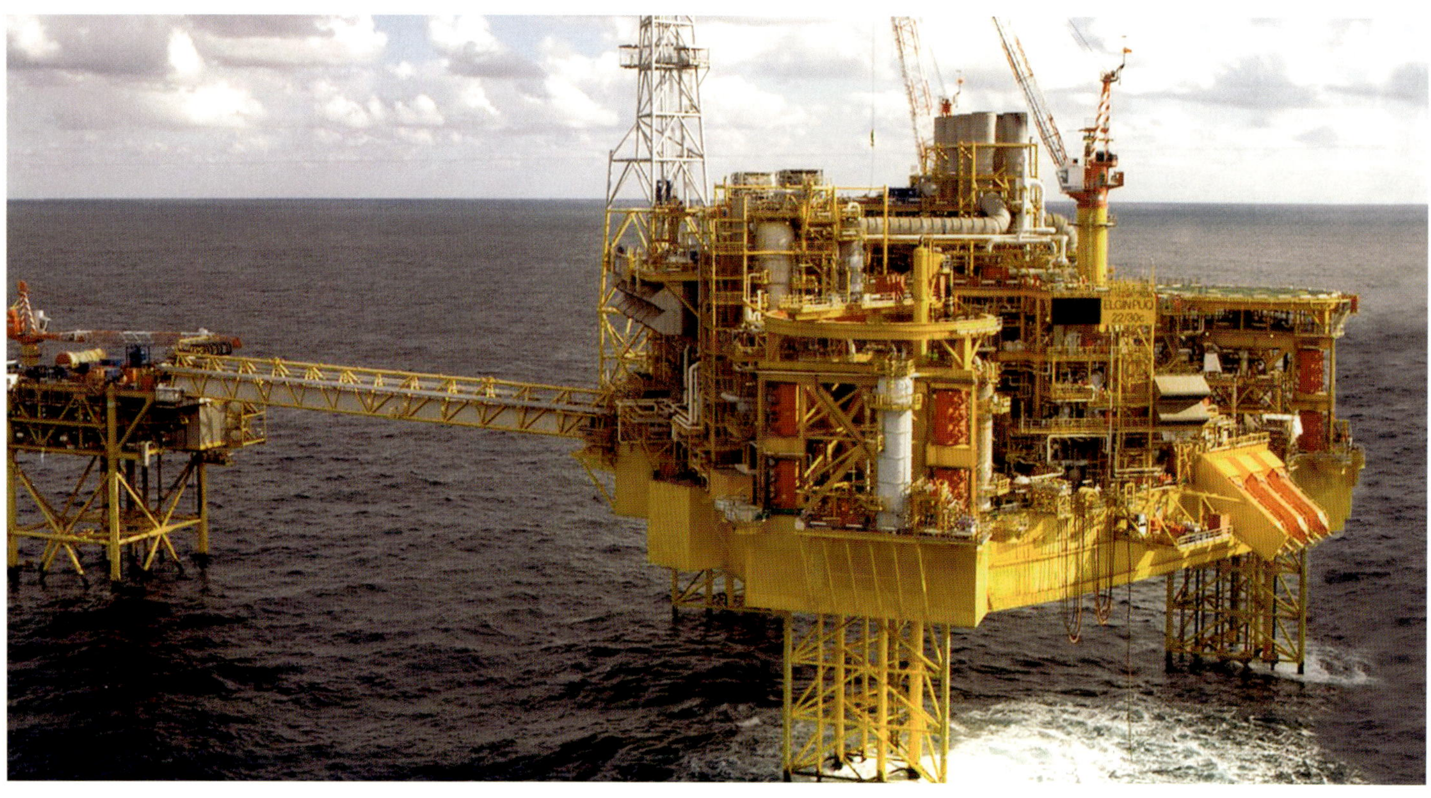

So firmly rooted now is the industry in Scottish society, scarcely a family circle is untouched; at it zenith 400 to 500 thousand people were employed around the UK. At the heart, Aberdeen and the north east, a stagnant economy hauled into the twentieth century and transformed into the energy capital of Europe, its debilitating migratory flood reversed by a dynamic mass of 900 new businesses. Against all the odds, with little tangible financial assistance and in a remarkably brief but frantic spell, small inexperienced local councils manufactured a miracle in new housing, roads, essential services, offices and industrial sites. Other areas, particularly the Highlands, responded similarly on a scale last experienced in wartime, but failed to capitalise by negotiating compensation for the upheaval. Only the stubborn islanders of Shetland and Orkney made their now legendary stand against Big Oil at the Sullom Voe and Flotta reception terminals and secured a financial birthright in revenues for future generations.

In all these Scottish communities, even around the fabrication sites (now deserted save one) there is only gratitude towards these standard bearers of a second industrial revolution. The transfusion of new blood and new ideas has permeated education, academic research and the arts, while an imported spirit of enterprise has spawned home-grown firms, now learning to reach out beyond the North Sea to deploy their hard-won talents throughout the world's emergent oil fields – a rebirth of Scotland's proud tradition of investing overseas.

The restless fossil fuel industry has a history of periodically reinventing itself in what is recognised as a mature declining province; heavy cost cutting and downsizing followed the rock bottom oil price scares in 1986 and 1999; a new environmental strategy emerged from Shell's Brent Spar decommissioning debacle; and, most dramatically and tragically, the Piper Alpha disaster in which 167 men died enforced a stringent new safety regime in an ever perilous milieu that had already claimed many other lives.

From the outset, frontiers have had to be constantly breached as the ingenious industry perfects new subsea wellhead and pipeline techniques, evolves innovative engineering and electronic systems, and constructs huge multi-purpose support vessels and adaptable rigs, in pursuit of the reluctant fifty per cent of hydrocarbons still believed trapped within the rocks under the North Sea, and to investigate promising areas west of Shetland, on the Atlantic Margin, where new problems lurk. Thus the UK province was literally the test bed for marine technologies now deployed as standard across the global industry. The Elgin-Franklin Field is an outstanding example, where Total's engineers have conquered the challenges of bringing into production high pressure and high temperature wells through the largest development of its kind in the world.

The original great operating companies and the contractors who now play a more major role remain heavily committed, while fresh rounds of exploration licenses have attracted independent newcomers and investors, all united in the belief that with the appropriate political and fiscal encouragement they can prolong an industry originally forecast to survive just twenty years. Four decades on, the men and women who operate a wiser and more mature industry steel themselves for challenges as formidable as those that confronted the stout pioneers who first voyaged north into the unknown.

[Left] **Total's Elgin-Franklin platform**

[Right] **Fionna Carlisle sketching at Sullom Voe, Shetland**

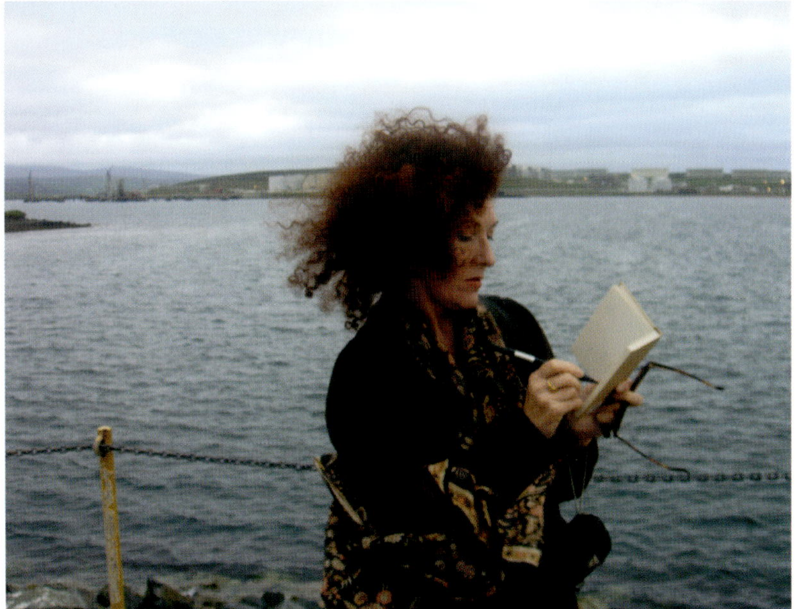

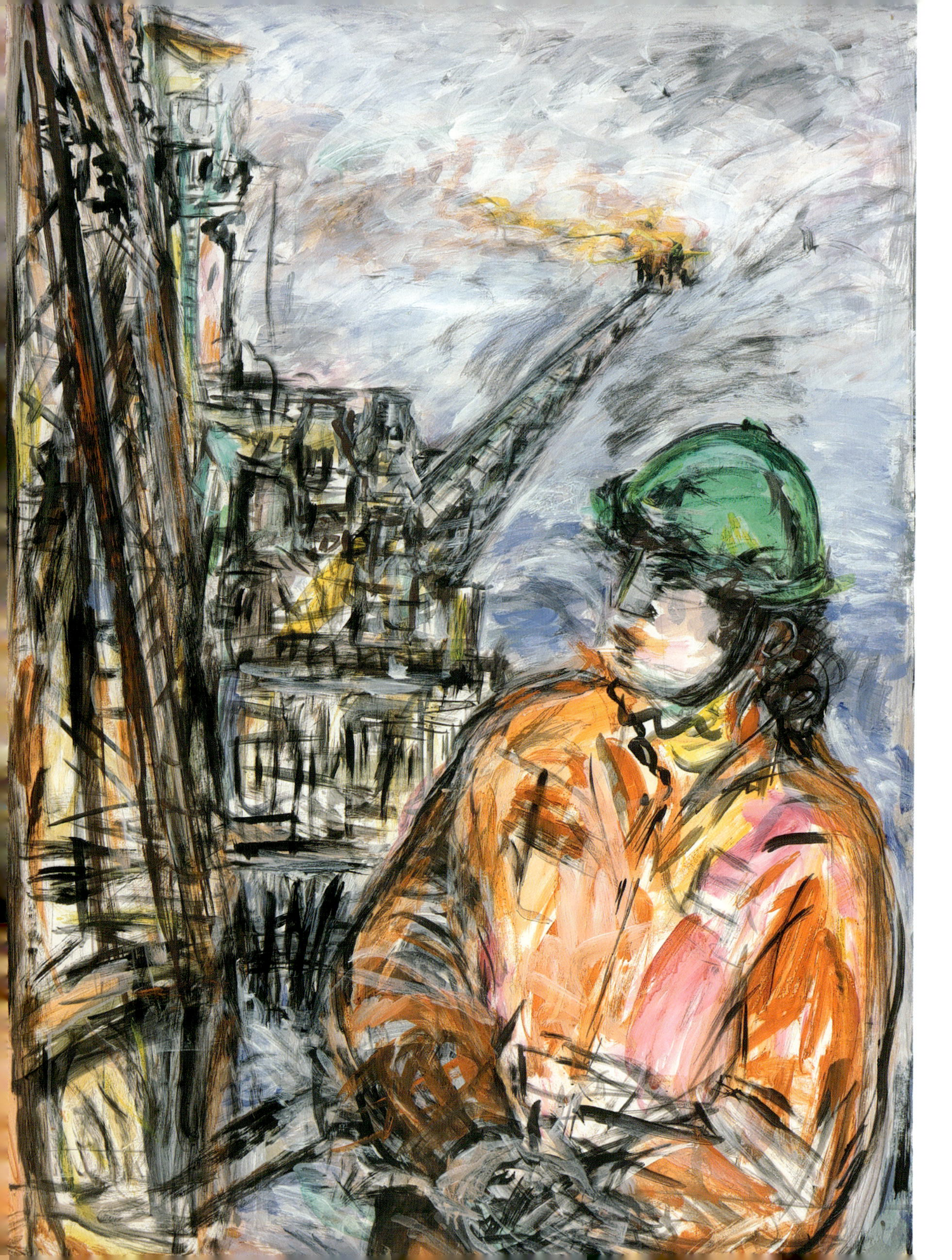

North Sea Portraits

DUNCAN MACMILLAN

Self-Portrait on Alwyn North, 2005
Painted in Xania, Greece · acrylic on paper, 150 x 115

It was in the 1970s that a dream became reality and extraction began of the oil discovered beneath the North Sea. Now more than forty years ago, that represents a whole generation. In the life of an individual that would mean maturity, recognition, even time for parenting perhaps; and that is what this exhibition marks. It is a coming of age. Many of the people recorded in these portraits have grown up and lived their working lives in the oil and gas industry of the North Sea. The new skills and new technologies developed here in Scotland in this difficult and dangerous environment have gone out across the world, and the people who developed them have gone with them. This is no longer just a local story. Aberdeen is now an international centre for the oil industry, but the success that this reflects has depended on the courage and ingenuity of individuals; the men and women who have gone out into one of the world's wildest seas to extract oil from deeper beneath the waves than anyone thought possible. It has been a great adventure. Those who have undertaken it have been true pioneers, facing difficulty and danger and working in extreme conditions. It is fitting to mark their achievement and to mark it as a human achievement, too, as the work of individuals, and that is what portraiture does. It celebrates the individual. This exhibition, *Energy: North Sea Portraits*, consists of twenty-four portraits by Fionna Carlisle of individual people from the industry. They are not just the 'suits' however, the men and women at the top; they are a cross-section, representative of the whole community that is the industry.

For it is a community. At once very diverse and very close, it is no longer just the preserve of a few big companies as it was at the beginning. They are still there of course – witness Total, who together with Arts & Business New Partners, are the generous sponsors of this project – but over forty years the whole character of the business has changed, part of the process of coming of age perhaps. As it has matured, and indeed as extraction has grown more difficult, demanding more expertise and more ingenuity, subcontracting to smaller companies has become the norm and individuals have often found it more profitable to market their skills or develop their ideas independently. It has become altogether a much more individualistic business. This exhibition reflects that development very clearly. There are almost as many different companies and organisations represented here as there are sitters.

It is in character therefore that this project also began with individual enterprise. It was not dreamt up in some corporate boardroom, nor was it the brainchild of a PR company. It was the product of the curiosity and initiative of the artist, Fionna Carlisle, herself. A native of Wick, Carlisle was familiar from childhood with the sea in all its moods and all its grandeur and had already painted it in a major series of dark and moody seascapes. She also had an established reputation as a portrait painter, however, and had painted a number of distinguished sitters before she embarked on this project. The late Robin Cook was among her subjects (that portrait now hangs in Portcullis House, House of Commons) and even while she was working on this series her portrait of the broadcaster and journalist, Sheena McDonald, was acquired by the Scottish National Portrait Gallery.

It was her background and her interest in the sea that first fired Carlisle's curiosity about the industry that had grown up in her lifetime out beyond the horizon. However, the first seeds of the project were sown in 2004, she says, when she was at a charity dinner in Aberdeen with leading figures from the oil industry, including Sir Ian Wood [p.33], head of the Wood Group. One of the most conspicuous examples of the success of individual entrepreneurial initiative, he was later to be the subject of a drawing in this collection. Andrew Hogg [p.36.], public affairs and corporate communication manager at Total,

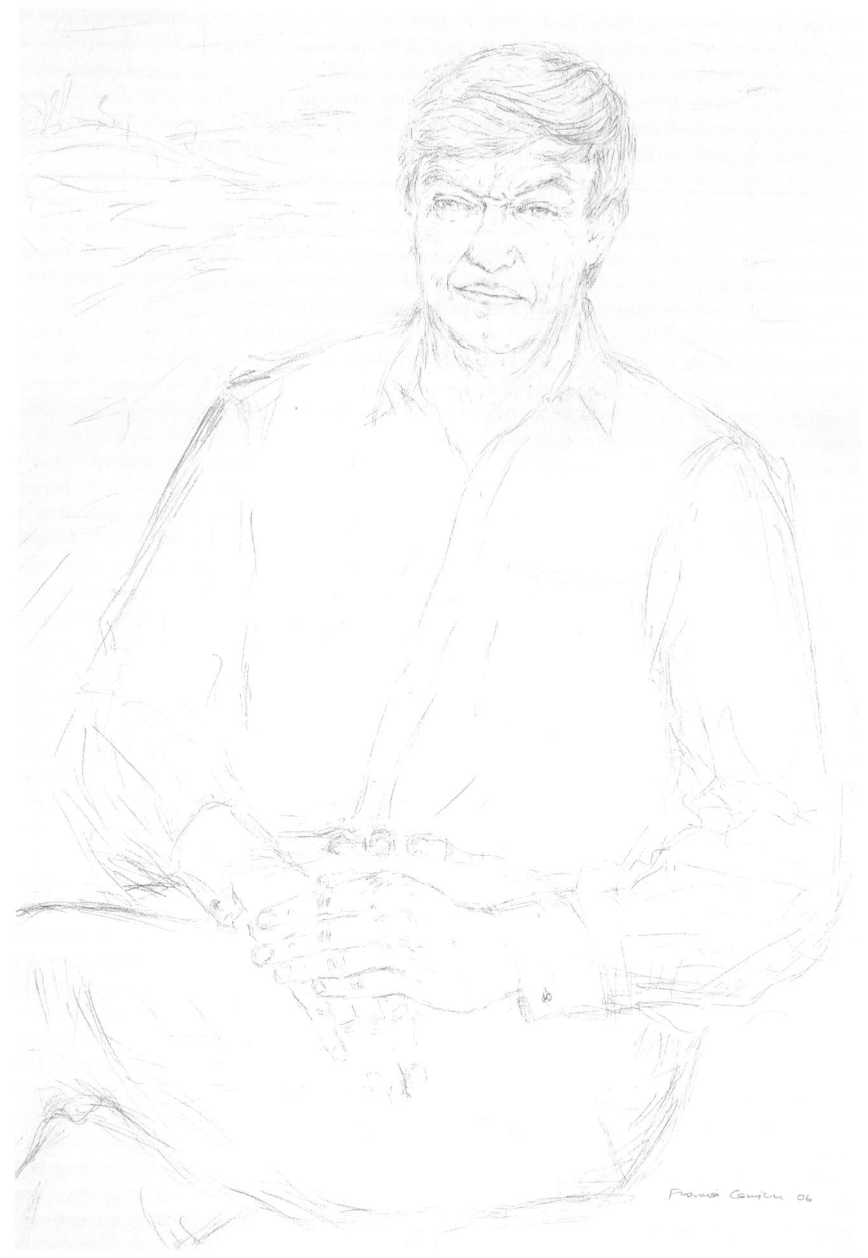

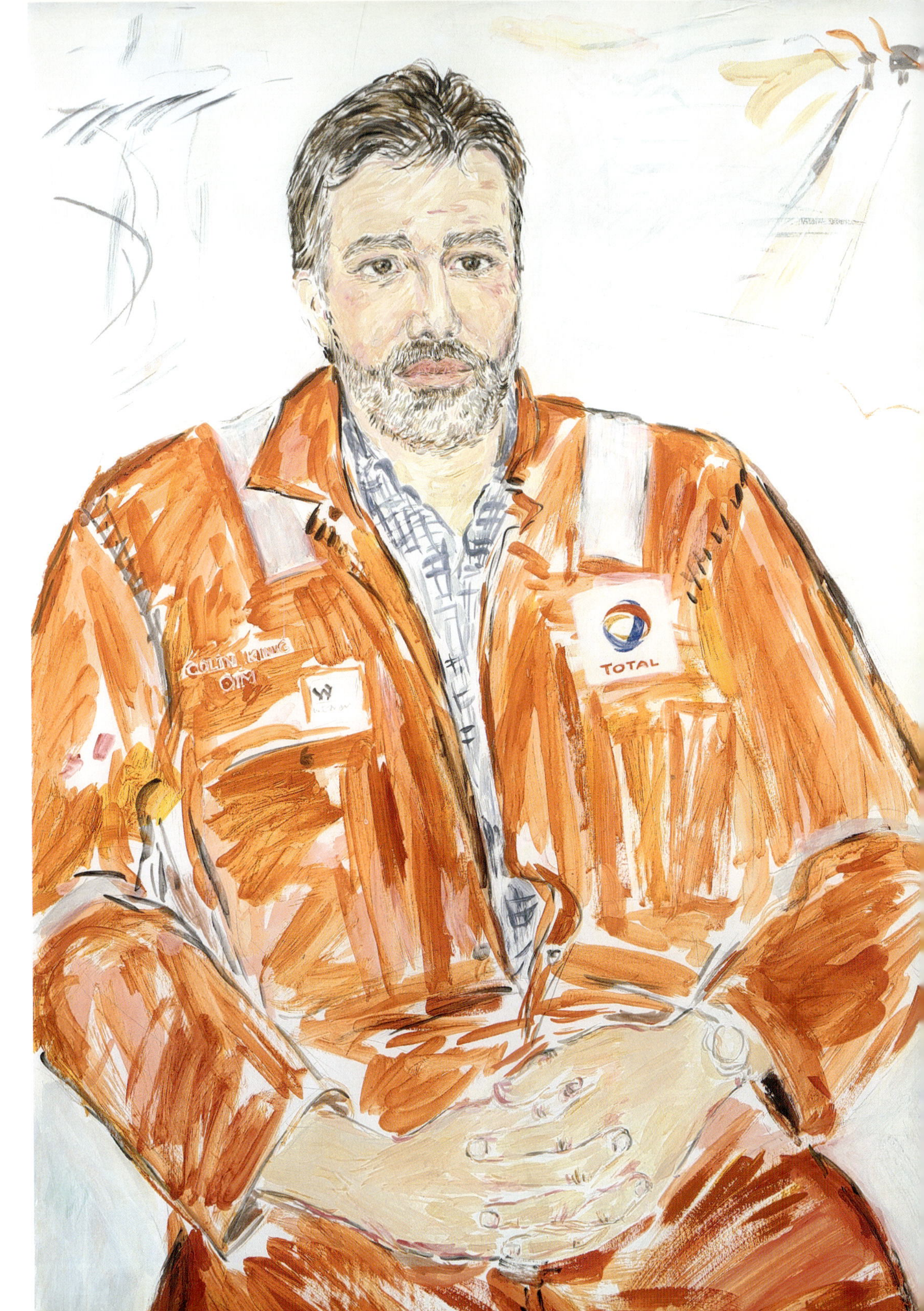

Michel Contie, Senior Vice-President Northern Europe & UK Country Representative, Total, 2006

Drawn in London · pencil on paper, 83.5 x 59.9

Colin King, Offshore Installation Manager (OIM), Alwyn North, Total, 2004

Painted on Alwyn North · acrylic on paper, 83.5 x 59.9

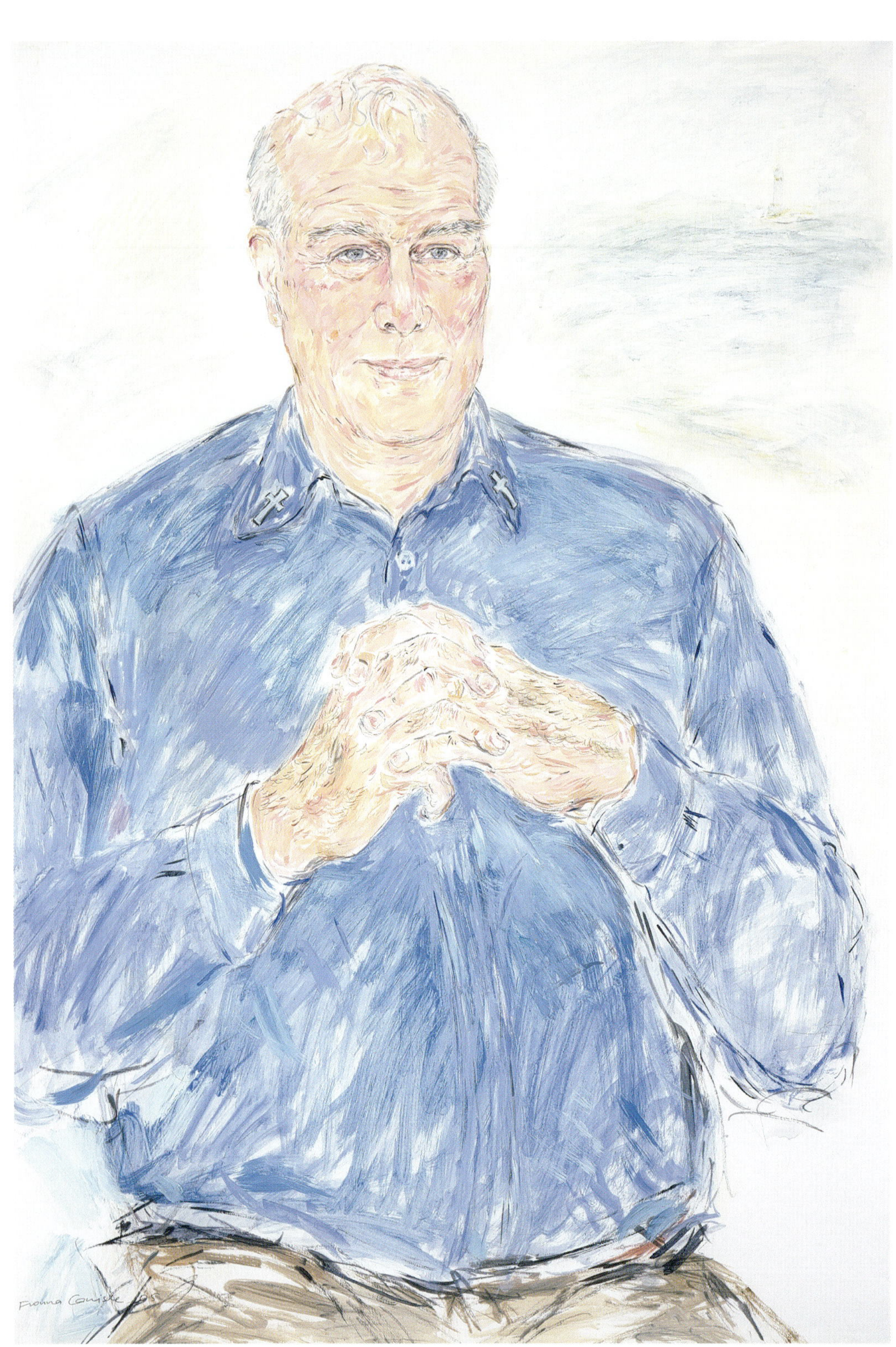

Reverend Angus Smith, Former Oil and Gas Industry Chaplain, 2005

Painted in Aberdeen · acrylic on paper, 83.5 x 59.9

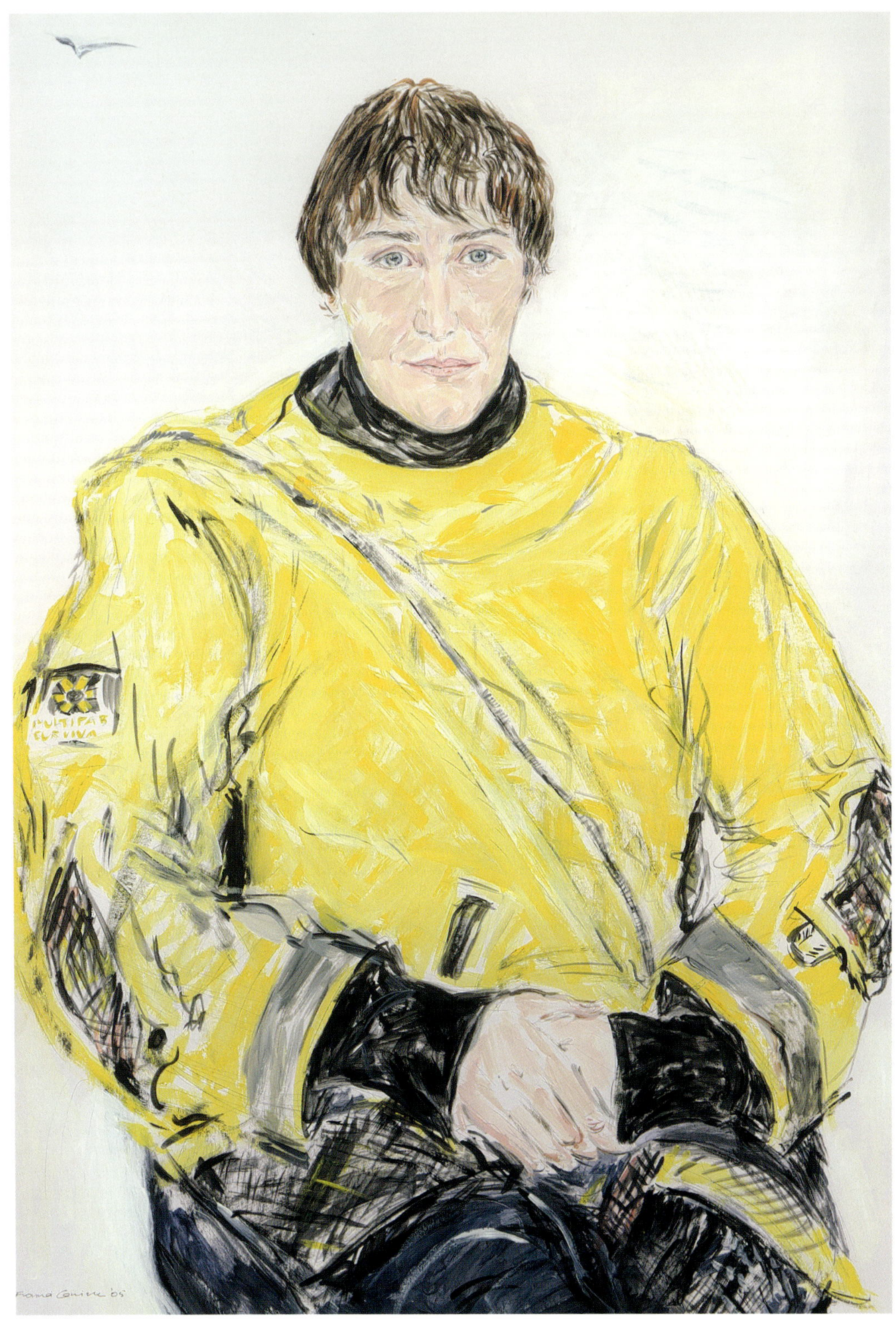

Laure Veyradier, Offshore Installation Manager (OIM), Elgin-Franklin, Total, 2005

Painted on Elgin-Franklin · acrylic on paper, 83.5 × 59.9

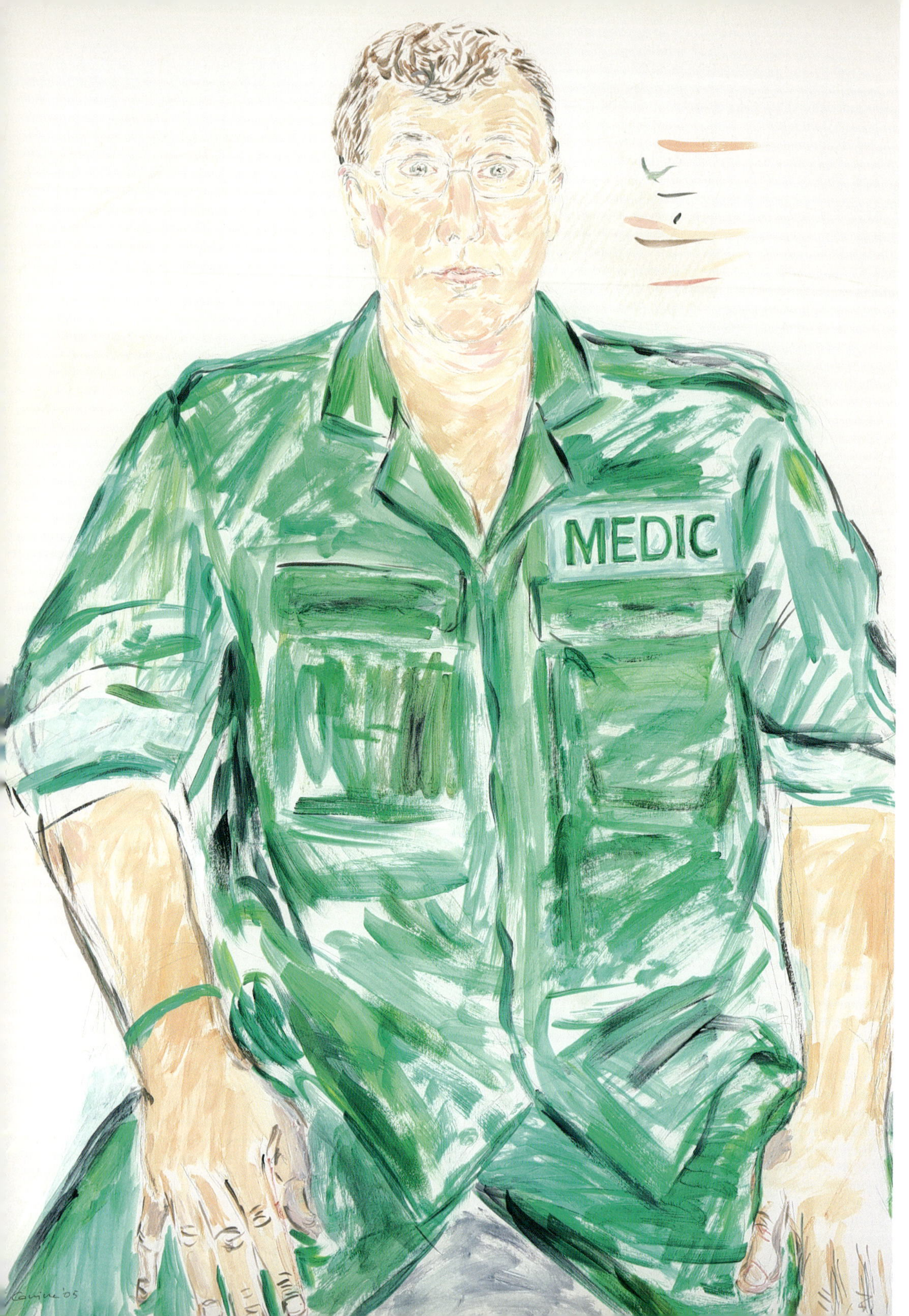

Neil Poole, Offshore Medic, Elgin-Franklin, Abermed Ltd, 2005
Painted on Elgin-Franklin · acrylic on paper, 83.5 x 59.9

Bill Edgar, Chairman of Subsea UK, President of The Institution of Mechanical Engineers, 2006
Painted in Aberdeen · acrylic on paper, 83.5 x 59.9

was there too. The artist was pleased to learn of Total's tradition of strong support for the arts. Intrigued by the oil industry and conscious that it had made so little impact artistically, she herself had been trying to find a way of visiting an oil platform. Their interests met. They kept in touch and eventually, in October 2004, she got the chance to go out to visit Total's Alwyn North oil platform.

When Carlisle set out, she had really no idea what she would do beyond drawing what she saw there. It was Sheena McDonald who advised her to take her easel; not that there was likely to be anywhere she could set it up in the confined space of an oil platform, but as a visible tool of her trade it would act as a token of her seriousness of purpose. She did use it however, and on that trip she made four portraits including most importantly that of Colin King [p.15], the offshore installation manager (OIM) of the platform, really the captain of the ship. She painted him wearing his orange safety overalls with his name and OIM badge prominently displayed on them. This portrait was an important step in establishing her credibility. She was fortunate in that when she arrived on the platform, King happened to have time to show her around. It was almost casually that she started to draw him when they were sitting in his office, but it was with that drawing that the project began.

She also drew rig superintendent Alan Paterson on that visit to Alwyn North. She usually draws her portraits before she paints

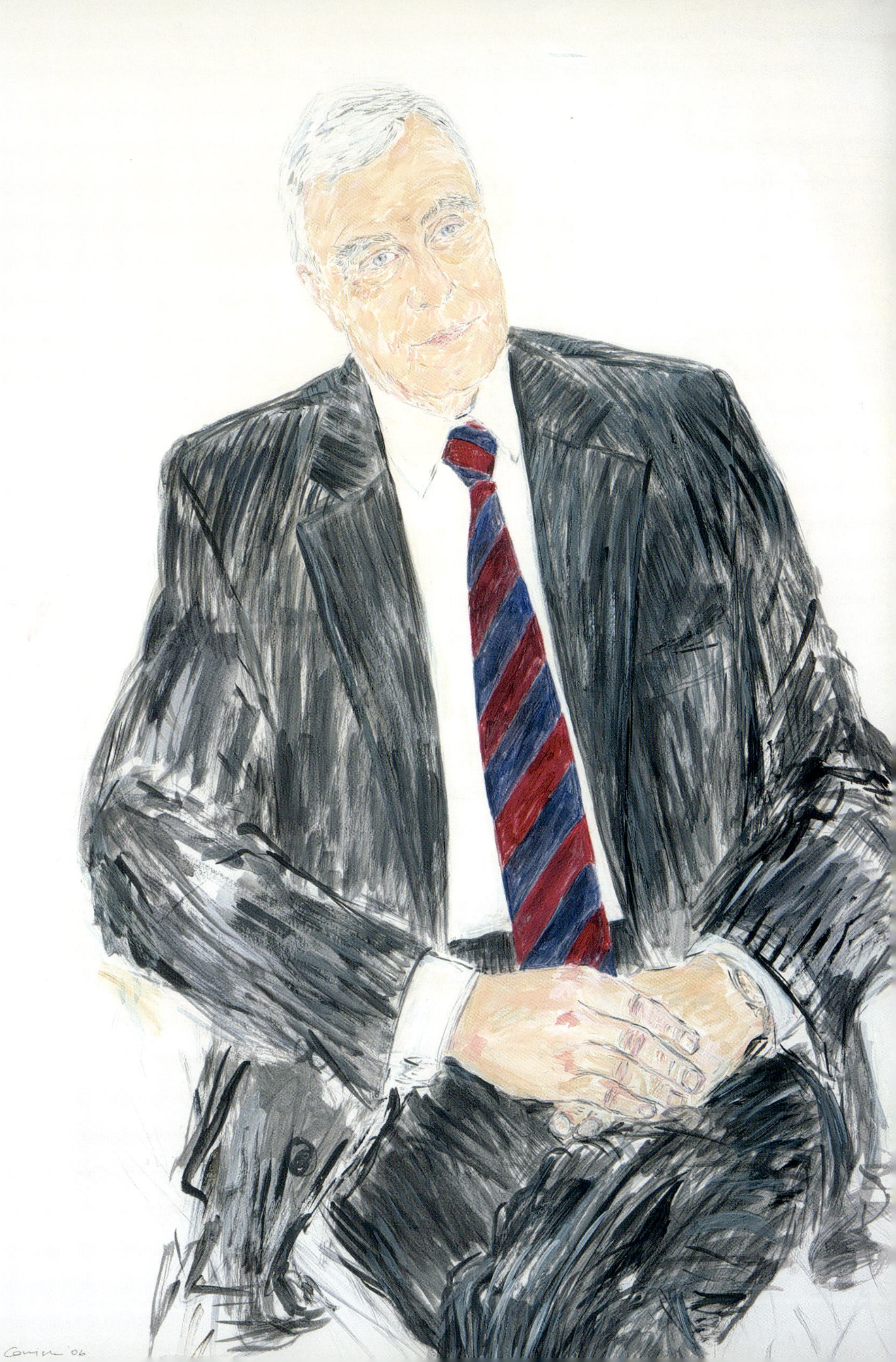

and, constrained by time, she was going to leave his as a simple drawing, but the sitter made it clear he would not consider it complete if his picture did not have colour as Colin King's portrait did. She had only two hours, but she did not want to disappoint him, so she did what she could in the time. That was typical of her experience. Her sitters were very quick to appreciate the significance of what she was doing and immediately saw the point of it. Robert Youngman [p.38], known as Rab the Rigger, also sat for her on that platform. The job of rigger is one of the toughest offshore and the depth of his experience is written in his face. When his friends teased him for sitting to her, a little bit out of keeping with his hard man image, his riposte was quick, emphatic and to the point, 'B***** off! You'll be sorry when I am in the Tate!'

With responses like this, Carlisle realised that she had found a new and exacting public. They had a clear idea of what they expected from her, but she would also have to learn to work fast if she was to fulfil their expectations. Nevertheless she was delighted at the way the people she met took her seriously. They certainly responded to her personal warmth and openness, but with the confidence that that generated they were able to take her as a professional, someone like them with a job to do and so going about her business as they were doing in the difficult and cramped circumstances that they all shared on the platform. Her first visit was seen as a great

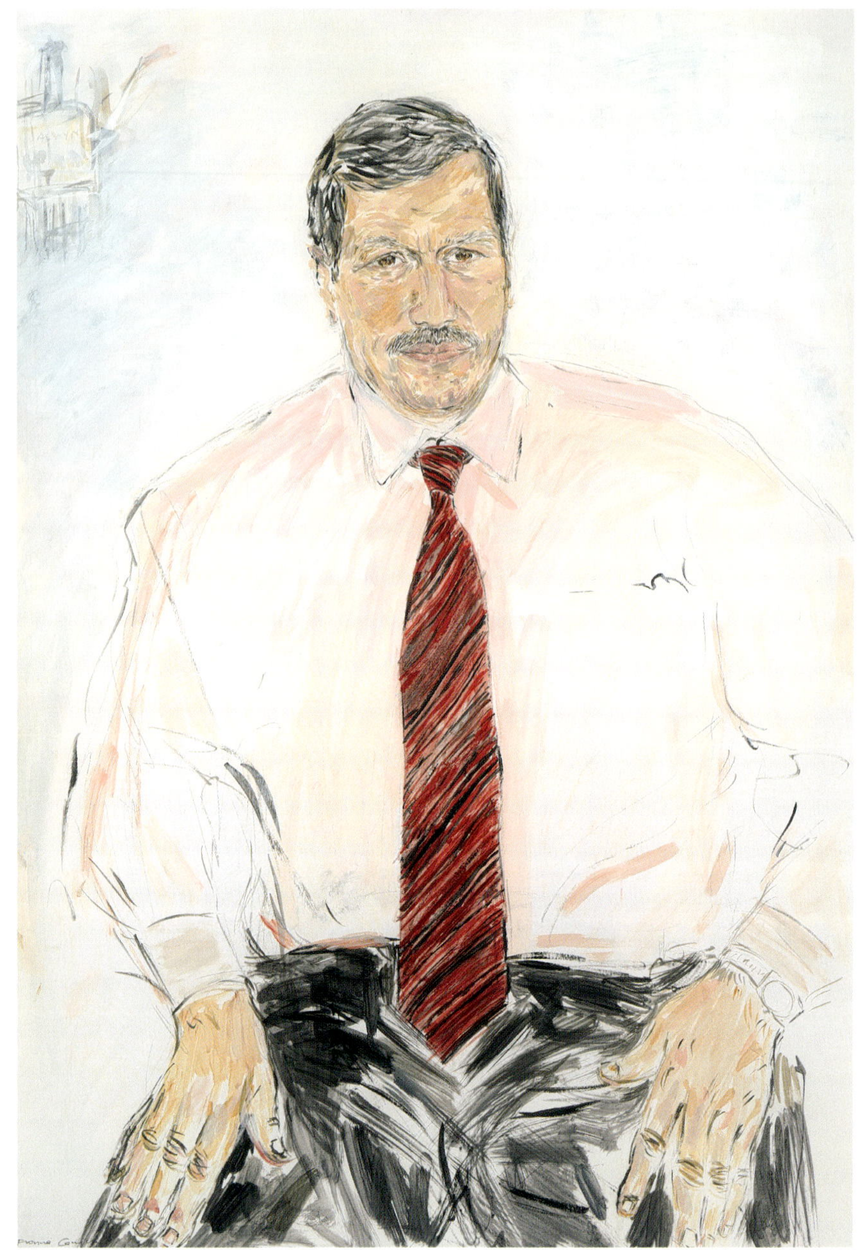

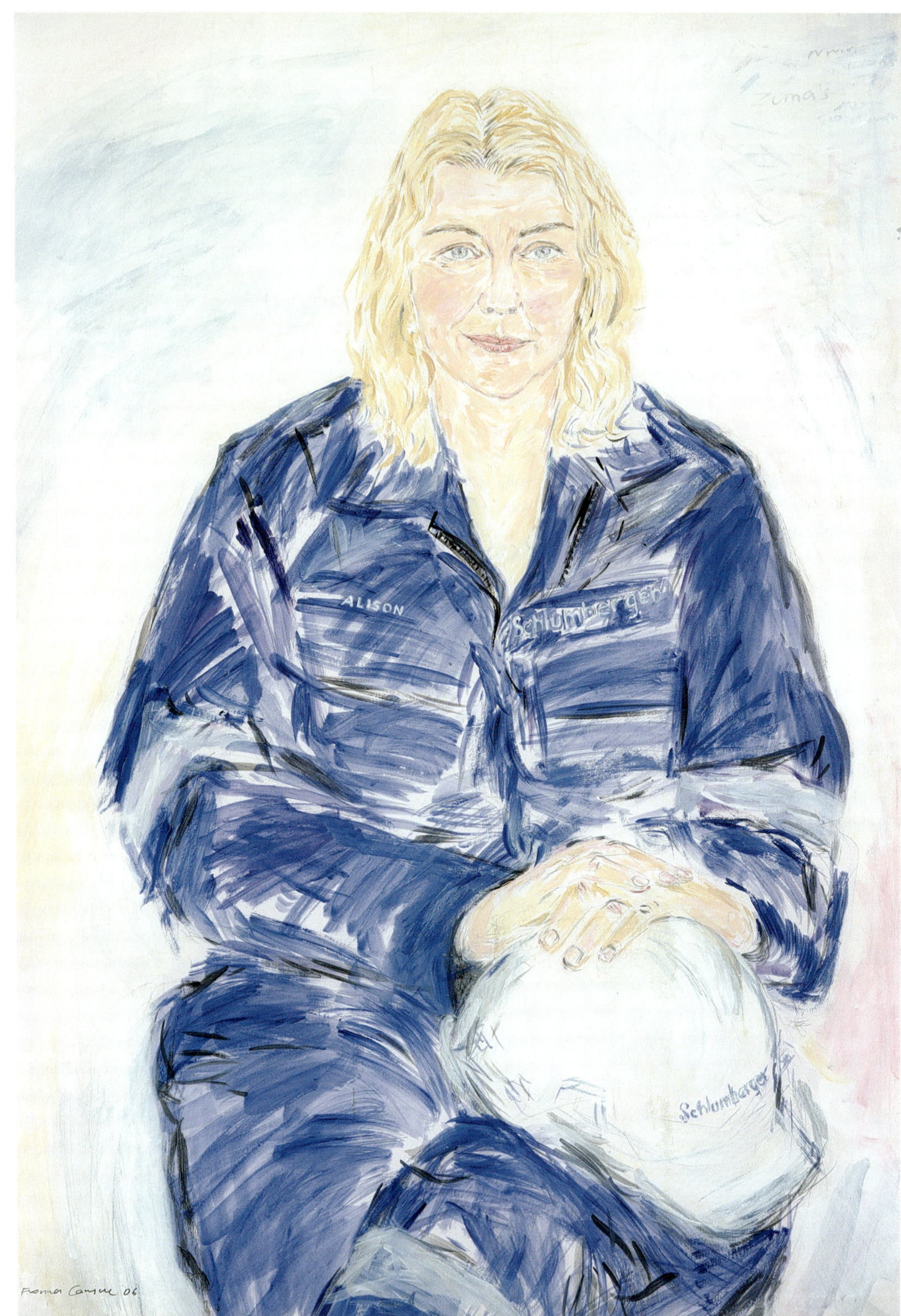

Syed Maqsood Sher, Group Operations Manager and Executive Vice-President, Orient Petroleum Company, 2005

Painted in Aberdeen · acrylic on paper, 83.5 x 59.9

Alison Goligher, Vice-President, Corporate Support Shell, 2006

Painted in Edinburgh · acrylic on paper, 83.5 x 59.9

success, both in what she had done, but also in the way the men and women on the platform had accepted her and her work. However problematic the purpose of art may have become 'on the beach', as offshore workers call the mainland, it seemed there was a job to be done offshore. It was to record and celebrate the people of the industry, the oil workers of Scotland. The project grew from there.

It remained very much the artist's own project, however. 'It has been up to me to charm people into posing,' Carlisle said, and those she charmed include the formidable managing director of Total E & P UK, Michel Contie [p.14] (now senior vice-president for Northern Europe), the man who managed the merger of Total and Elf's UK North Sea businesses, though he only had time to sit for a drawing and he was exacting with the arrangements even for that. She has captured his energy and impatience in her drawing of him as he sits in an open-necked shirt, but he was disarmed nevertheless. He sat for much longer than planned and gave the project his blessing. He also confirmed her own instinct that this should be more than a collection of board-room portraits and indeed that it should reflect the diversity of the whole industry and not just Total's part in it. He also wanted its international character to be reflected in the people she painted. In keeping with that, his own recommendation for inclusion in the portraits was the imposing figure of Maqsood Sher [p.20] with whom he had worked in South America. At the time Maqsood Sher was offshore operations manager for Total in Aberdeen. Sher saw immediately the value of the project, commenting that 'the artist is very important to society' and his support was important for Fionna's platform visits. There are other senior figures included, too. Bill Edgar [p.19], formerly managing director of the John Wood Group PLC and now chairman of Subsea UK is included, as is the politician, Alex Salmond [p.29]. However, all the sitters are treated as equals and with the same engaging informality. Altogether it is an international group too. There are a number of French people, but not simply because Total is a French firm. Galley boss on Alwyn North, Joseph Lahbib [p.32], who went offshore from a job at Gleneagles Hotel, for instance, is French, but is a long-time resident in Scotland. The weeks-on-weeks-off schedule offshore was better for family life than the relentless hours of the hotel, he reckoned. Another sitter is John Bey [p.25] whose family claim Turkish origin. He was the artist's companion in the office that she used as a studio on Alwyn North.

It was a formidable task that Carlisle had undertaken, however. She had to be her own administrator, arranging all her meetings and sittings and liaising both with onshore and offshore contacts. Going offshore was far from easy, too. Helicopters are not airliners. Spending two or three hours in a washing machine was how she described it. It is very

Lord (William Douglas) Cullen of Whitekirk, 2006
Painted in Edinburgh · acrylic on paper, 175 x 98.5

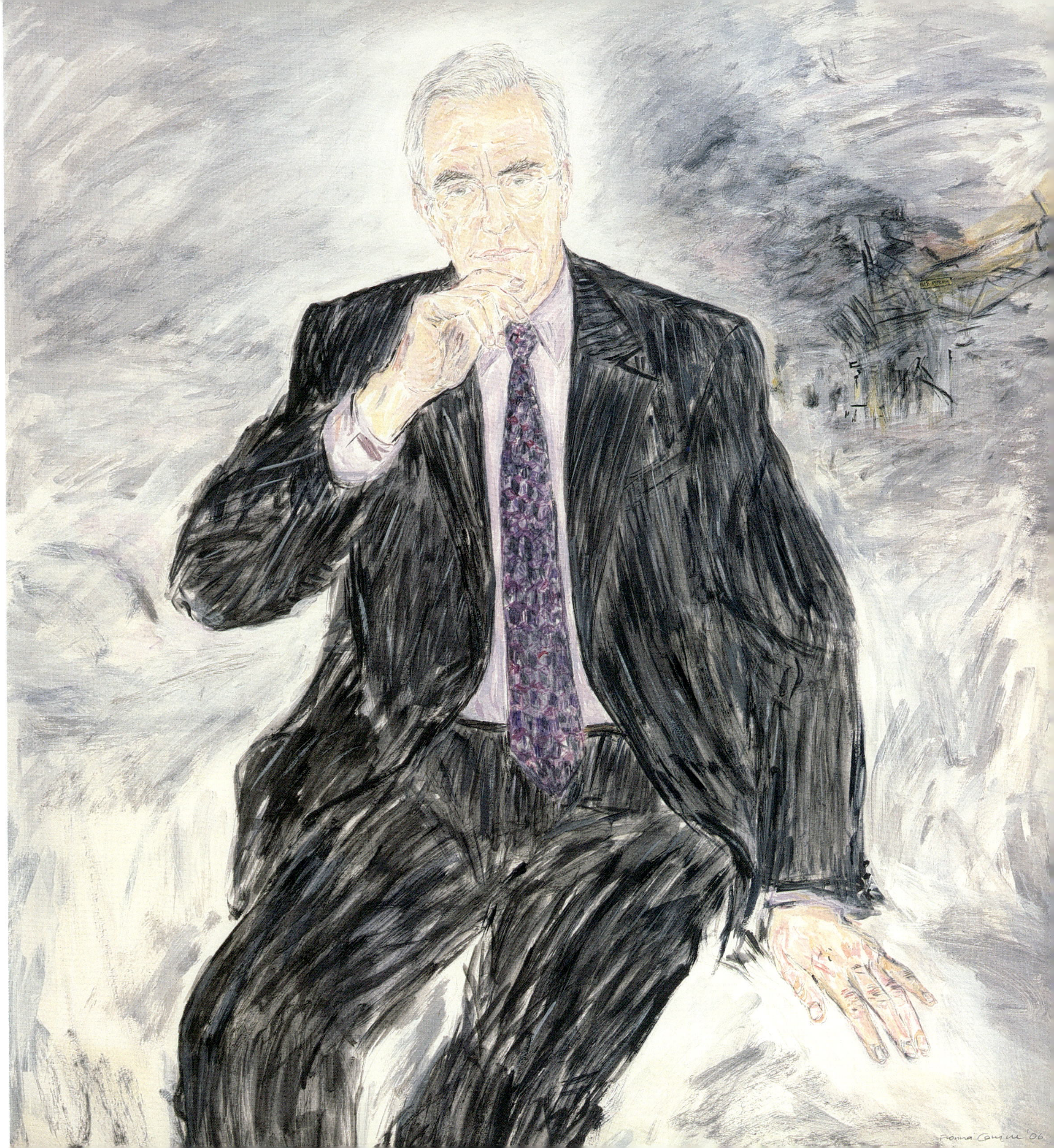

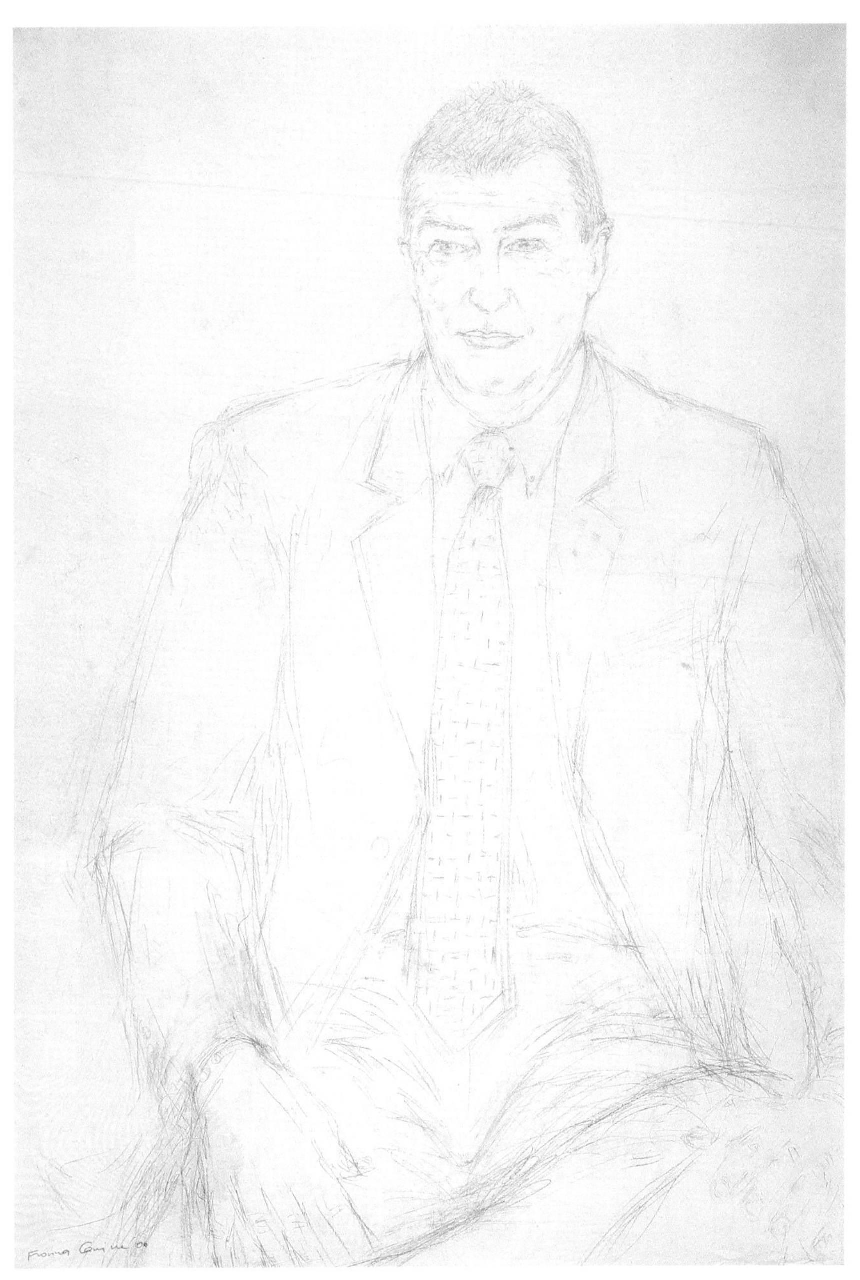

John Burns, Head of Operations,
St Fergus Gas Terminal, Total, 2006
Drawn at St Fergus Gas Terminal
Pencil on paper, 83.5 x 59.9

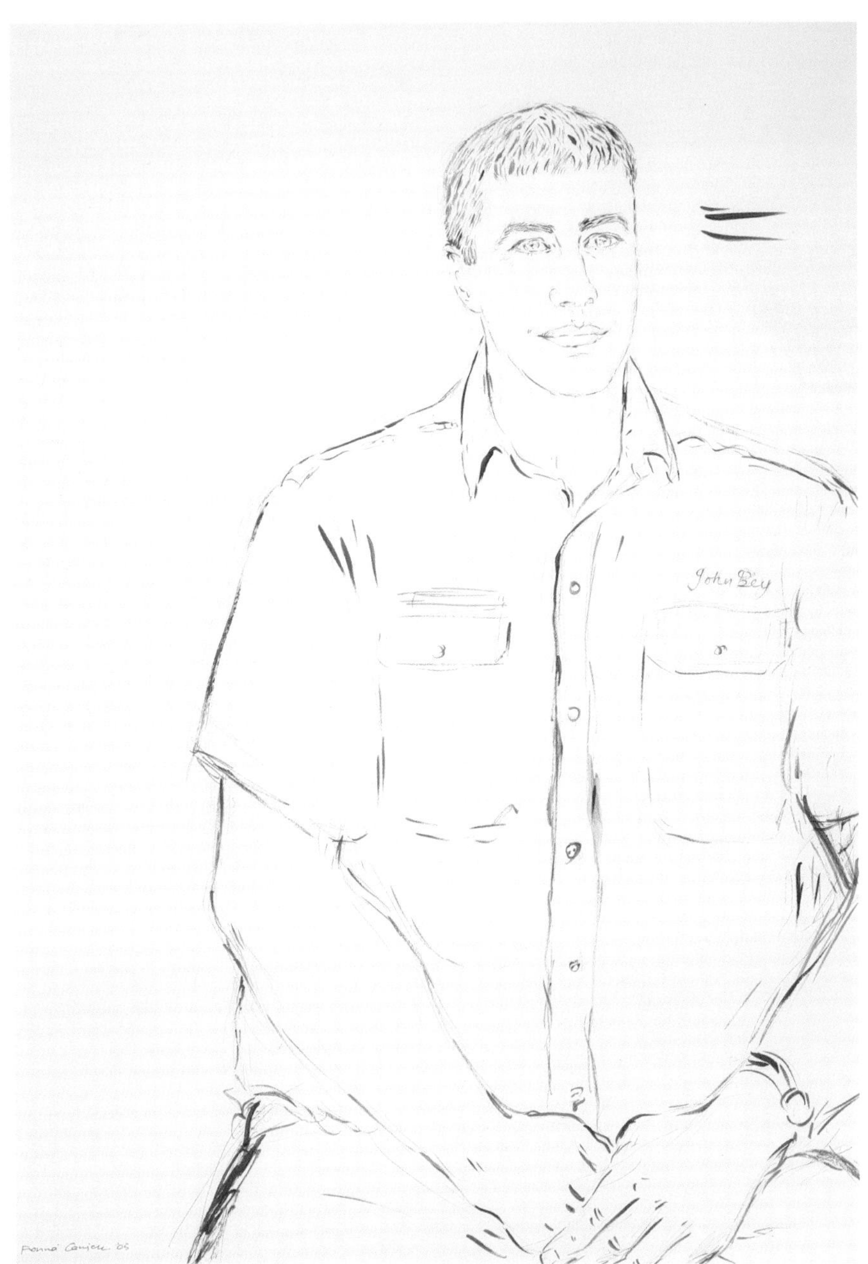

John Bey, Control Room Operator,
Alwyn North, Total, 2005
Painted on Alwyn North
Acrylic on paper, 83.5 x 59.9

uncomfortable being jiggled up and down for several hours, without access to a loo, strapped tightly in and wearing a heavy yellow survival suit. She has painted one of her sitters, Laure Veyradier [p.17], one of the first women OIMs in the North Sea sector, in her survival suit. That was how they first met, both wearing yellow suits as they waited to board the helicopter that would take them to the Elgin-Franklin platform. She has also recorded in sketches the figures of those around her on the helicopter, all sleeping, in spite of the discomfort, lulled to sleep by the rhythmic pulse of the rotor blades.

Elgin-Franklin was the second platform the artist visited. She made four trips offshore in all, two to Alwyn North, in October 2004 and November 2005 and two to Elgin-Franklin towards the end of 2005. After her first trip, the rules required that before she could make a second visit offshore, she had to undergo full safety training – nothing less than an ordeal by fire and water. It meant going through various stages of difficult underwater escapes until finally she had to escape from an upside-down helicopter submerged in a tank. She also had to walk through fire. But she would not have been so successful in the record she has made if she had not been willing to submit to such ordeals and so show herself as tough and courageous as those she records. Among them, one of the toughest looking is safety specialist, David McKeon [p.39]. Called the Silver Fox because of his long grey hair, he

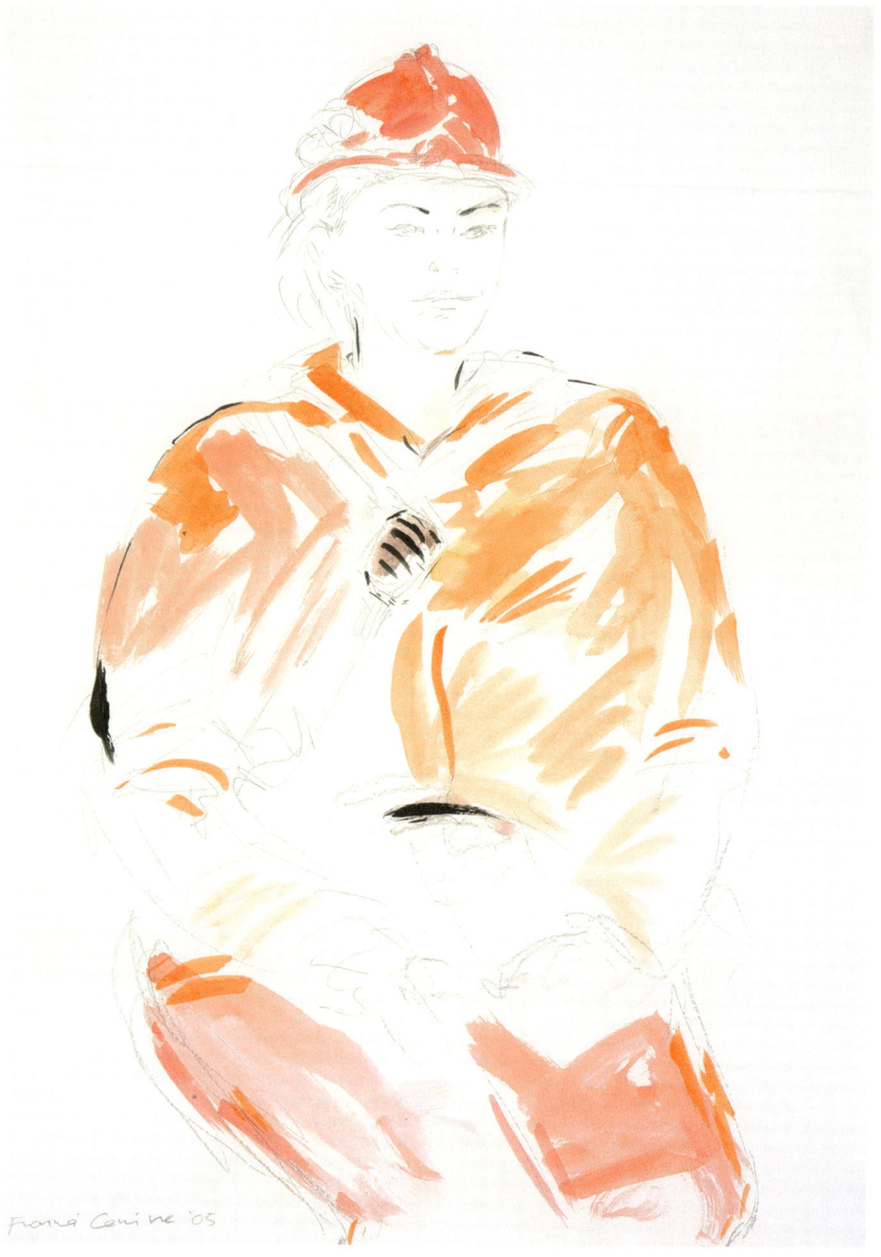

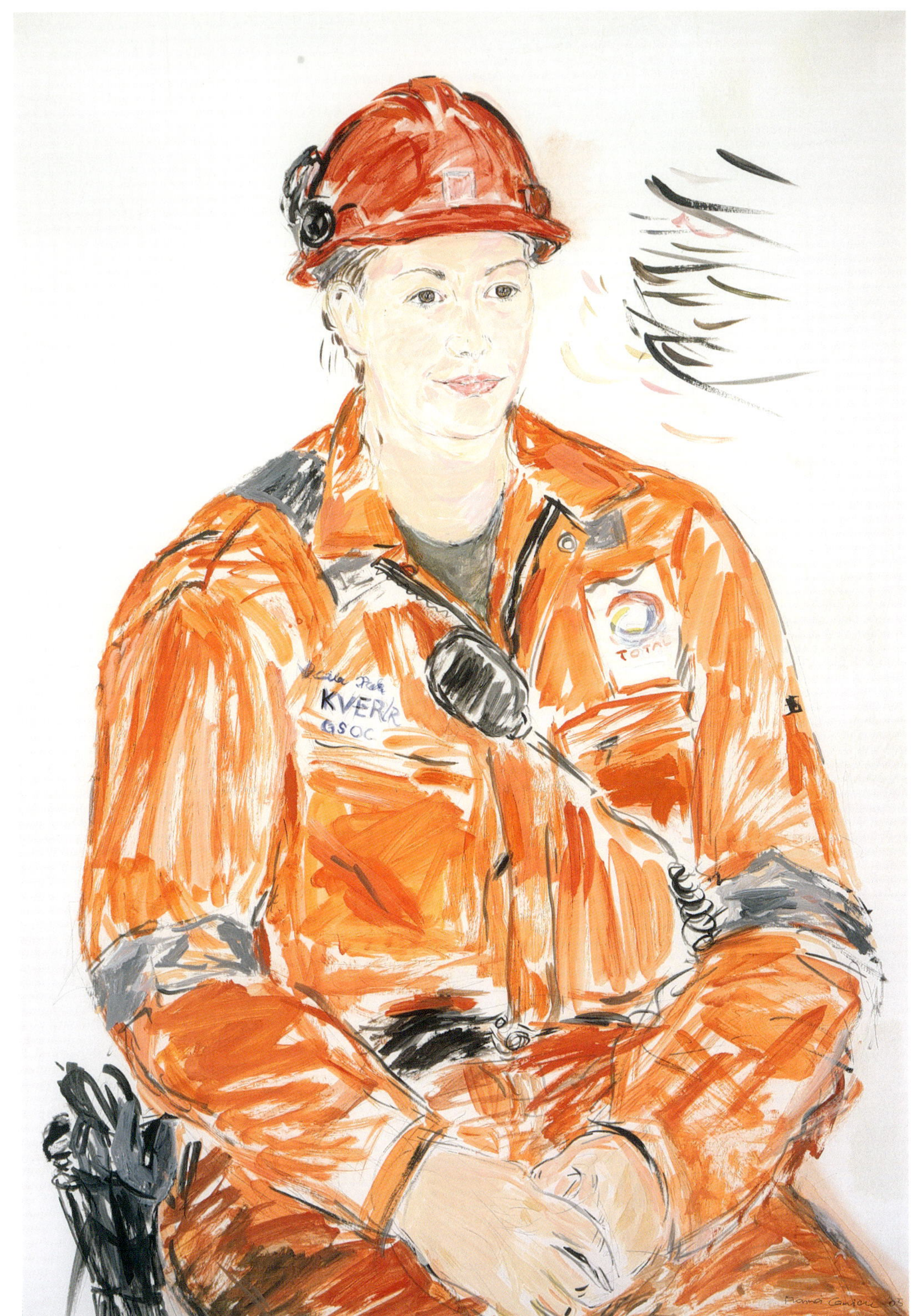

Preliminary sketch for Nicola Park, Control Room Operator, St Fergus Gas Terminal, AkerKvaerner Offshore Partner Ltd, 2005

Painted at St Fergus Gas Terminal · watercolour on paper, 42 x 29.7

Nicola Park, Control Room Operator, St Fergus Gas Terminal, AkerKvaerner Offshore Partner Ltd, 2005

Painted at St Fergus Gas Terminal · acrylic on paper, 83.5 x 59.9

is from the safety organisation, Rubicon Response Ltd, and is in charge of fire fighting on the safety induction course. He disconcerted the artist by growing a beard between sittings.

Conditions on the platforms were difficult. Inside it can be confined and there are few windows. Outside on the decks it is dangerous. She was not allowed outside alone until she was deemed sufficiently experienced, and always had to borrow space to work. But she had to adapt to such things. Circumstances forced her development just as the difficulties of the North Sea itself accelerated development of the processes of exploration and extraction. She used to work slowly, requiring many sittings, but limited space and limited time, both of her own presence offshore and in her sitters' busy schedules, made her change her habits. Her work is lighter and quicker now, though in its way no less finished. Looking at it, hearing her speak of her experience and hearing others describe their response to her, one is reminded that portraiture is essentially a social business. It flourishes in that intuitive space where we are defined as individuals by those around us. It is a space that the camera cannot occupy; because it is merely mechanical, it cannot participate in the social exchange which produces the painted portrait. It is no accident that both Raeburn and Ramsay, the two greatest Scottish portrait painters, were men of great warmth and naturalness of manner. They put their sitters at their ease. She has that same gift.

In these portraits she has used a common format. The only exceptions are her portrait of Andrew Hogg and also her own self-portrait [p.12]. Otherwise all her subjects are seated, three-quarter length with the heads in the same position within the frame and facing the viewer directly. The hands are visible, but not the chairs that support the sitters. Instead they are framed and visually supported by the white paper background. It suggests a space, but does not define it. In a number of examples she has put something in the background, but it is never more than a hint. Lord Cullen [p.23], for instance, has, at his request, the image of Piper Alpha behind him, as he sits, hand to chin in a gesture of forensic reflection. Reverend Angus Smith [p.16], then oil and gas industry chaplain, has a lighthouse just visible behind him, a spiritual beacon perhaps.

Carlisle has achieved good likenesses, not only in the faces, but in the body language too, so her sitters each have a very strong, individual presence. You see that even more when you see them as a group. Then you really feel you are in the presence of a distinct community composed of strong individuals. The diversity she has achieved within the unity of a common format is reinforced, too, by the range of different costumes her sitters wear. She has made a feature out of the bright colours of their overalls, counter-pointed by the occasional dark suit. Altogether it is a

Alex Salmond, Leader of the Scottish National Party, Member of Parliament for Banff and Buchan, and Oil Economist, 2006
Painted at the House of Commons, London
Acrylic on paper, 83.5 x 59.9

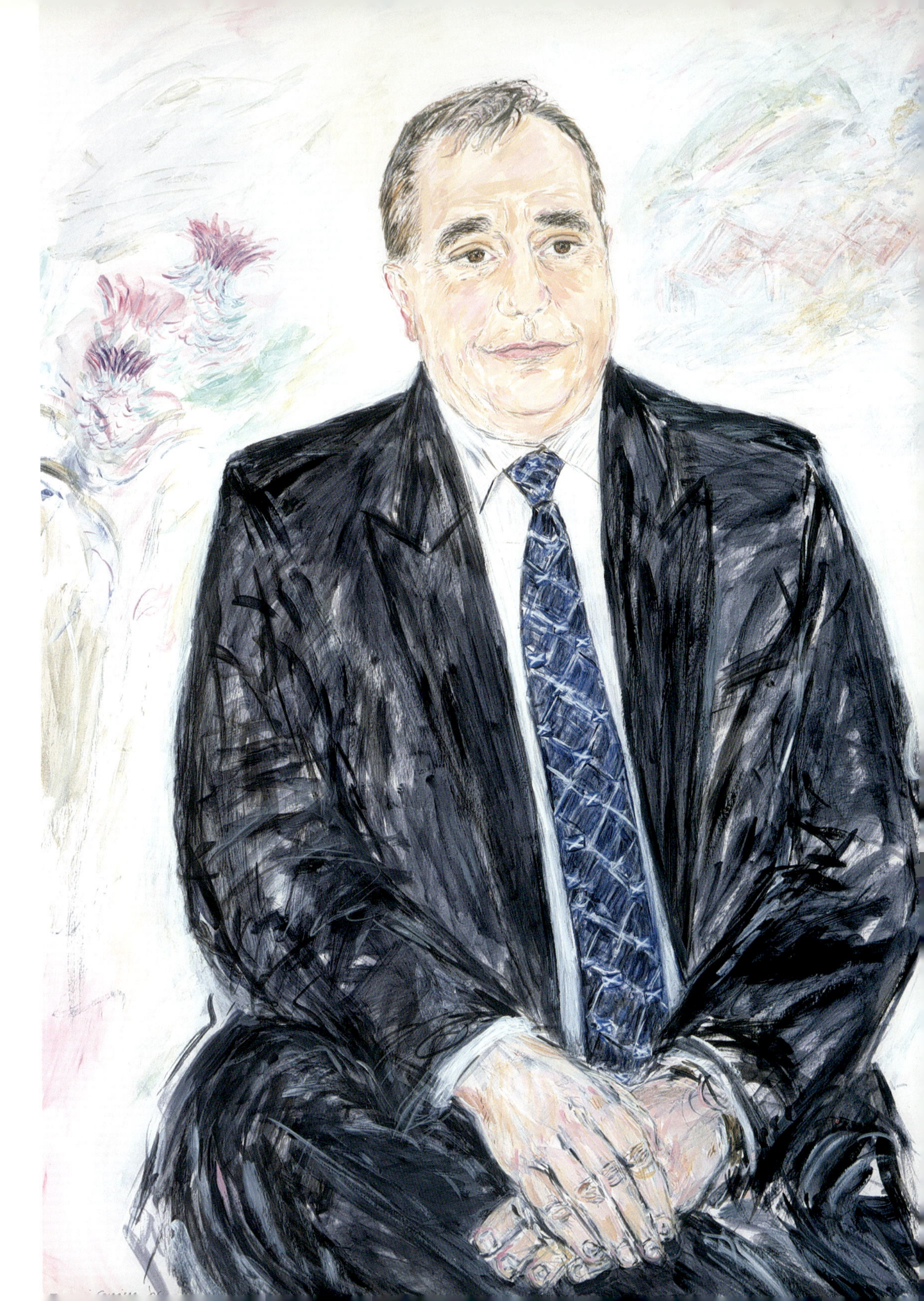

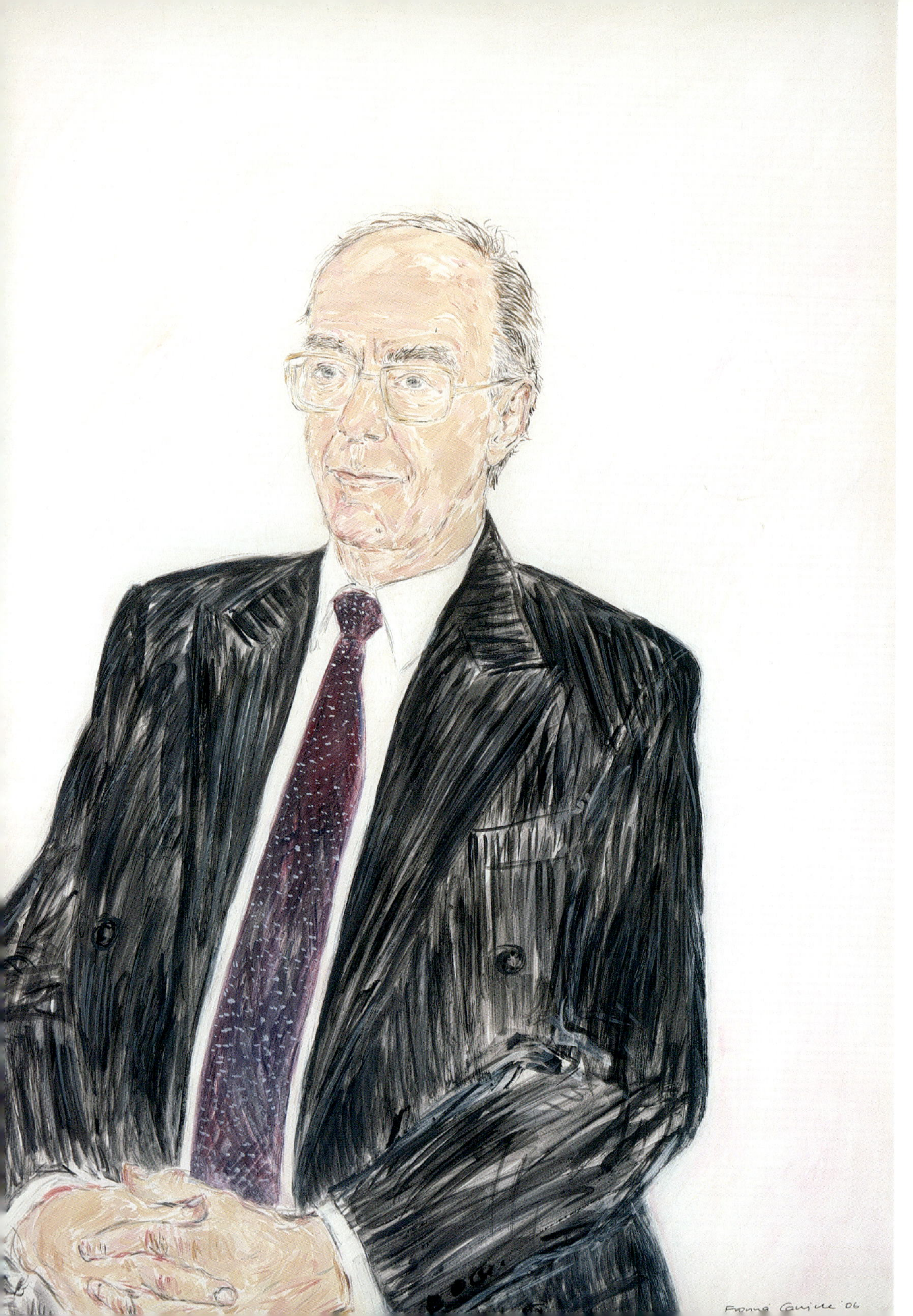

Alex Kemp, Professor of Petroleum Economics, University of Aberdeen, 2006

Painted in Aberdeen · acrylic on paper, 83.5 x 59.9

Jennifer Wink, Administration Supervisor, St Fergus Gas Terminal, Total, 2006

Painted at St Fergus Gas Terminal

Acrylic on paper, 83.5 x 59.9

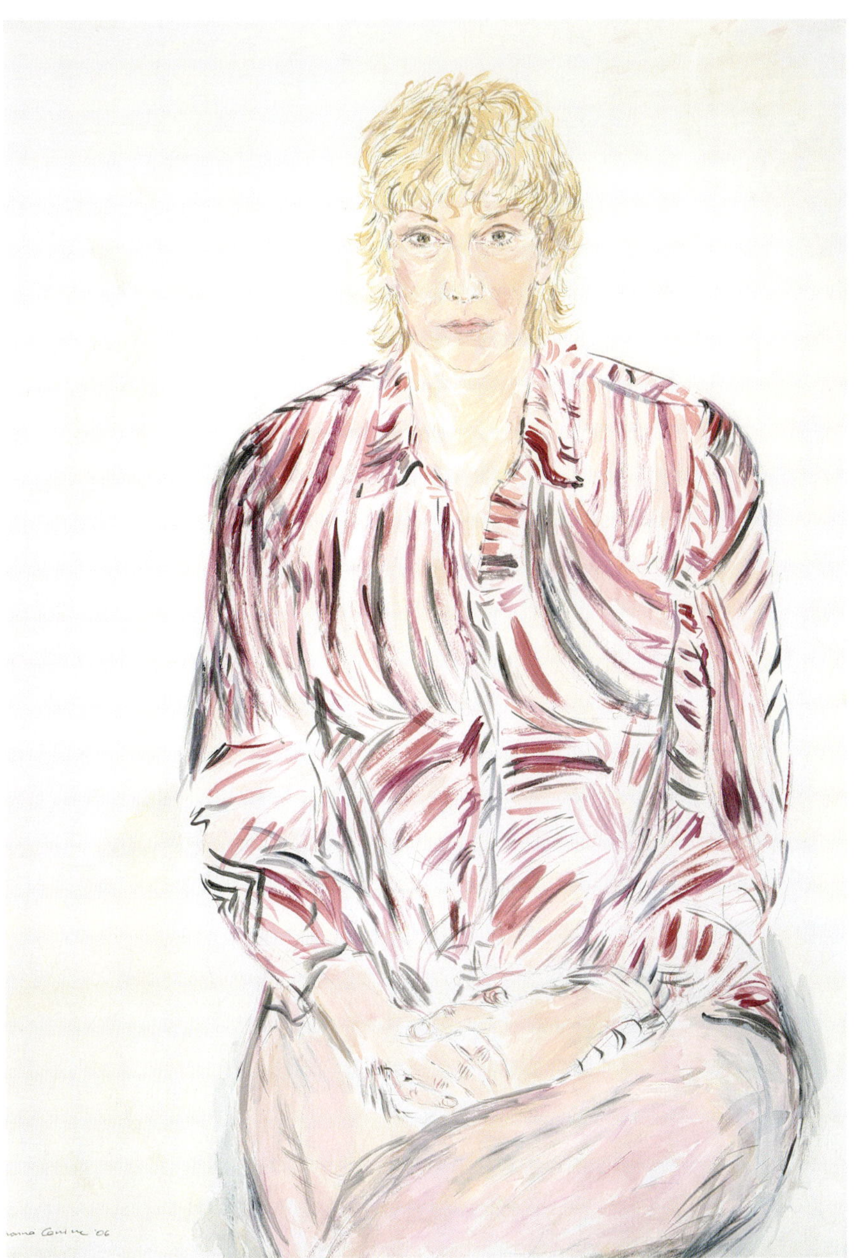

remarkable achievement. It is difficult to think of a comparable group of portraits working together to such effect. There is certainly little comparable in contemporary portraiture. You have to look back to much earlier examples like Sir John Medina's thirty-two portraits of the fellows of the Royal College of Surgeons painted between 1697 and 1708, to find a comparison. Notably, at the invitation of the surgeons Medina's own self-portrait was included in the series as hers is here.

Carlisle's portraits are all easy and natural. Her chosen technique of acrylic on paper adds to that effect. She never pushes it to a high finish, and details are suggested, but not dwelt on. Socially, we do not use detail as we observe each other. We intuitively register things like expression and body language and she has captured these brilliantly. She leaves the movement of her brush clearly visible so that we follow her hand as it explores and records what she sees.

Good portraiture has to strike a balance between our intuitive sense of continuity and permanence and our equally strong – it is deeper though less present perhaps – sense of the mutability and impermanence of all things and most of all of human life. In the twenty-first century, especially in the uncertain world we inhabit, the intuitive certainty that gives such strength to Raeburn's art, a perfect balance of the permanent and the impermanent, could not be available to a portrait painter. Were Fionna Carlisle to attempt it, we

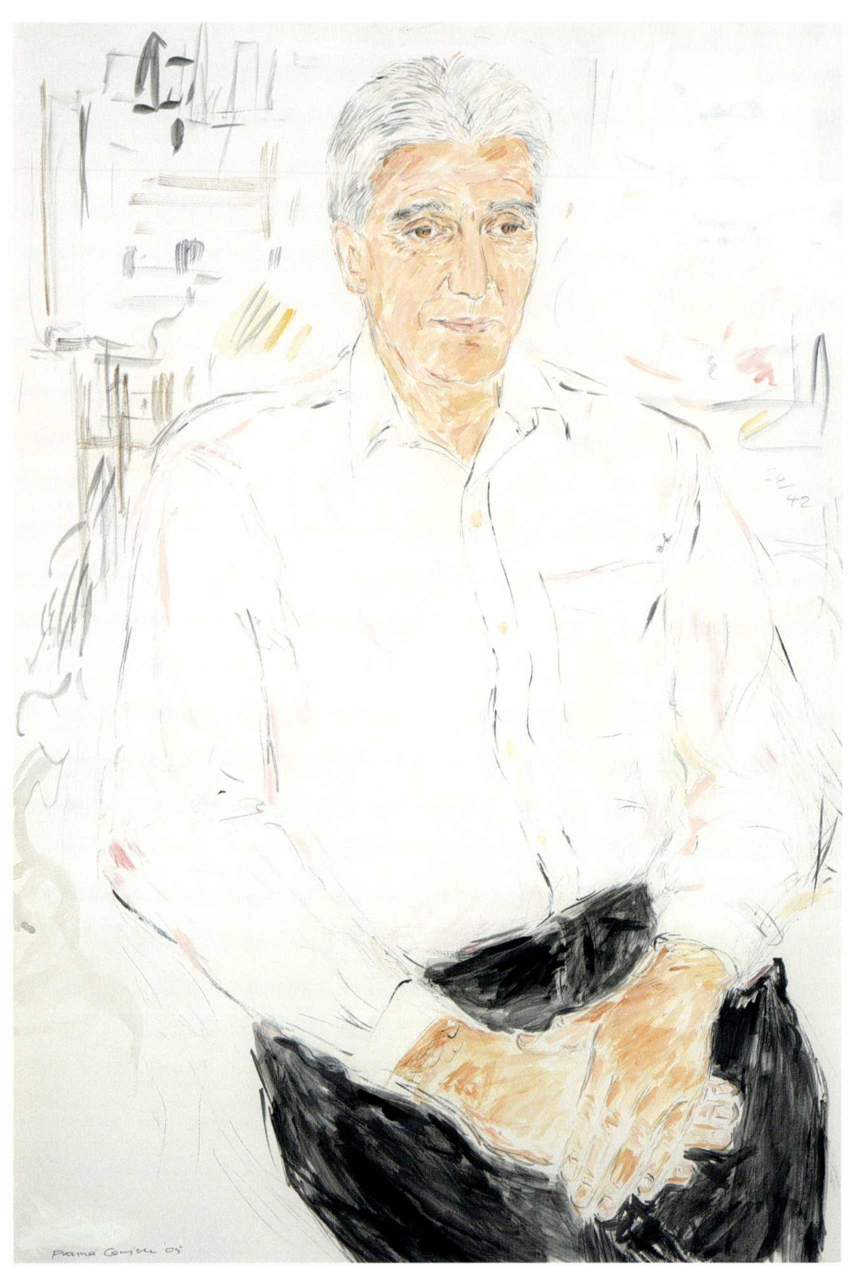

Joseph Lahbib, Catering Facilites Manager, Alwyn North, Total, 2005

Painted on Alwyn North · acrylic on paper, 83.5 x 59.9

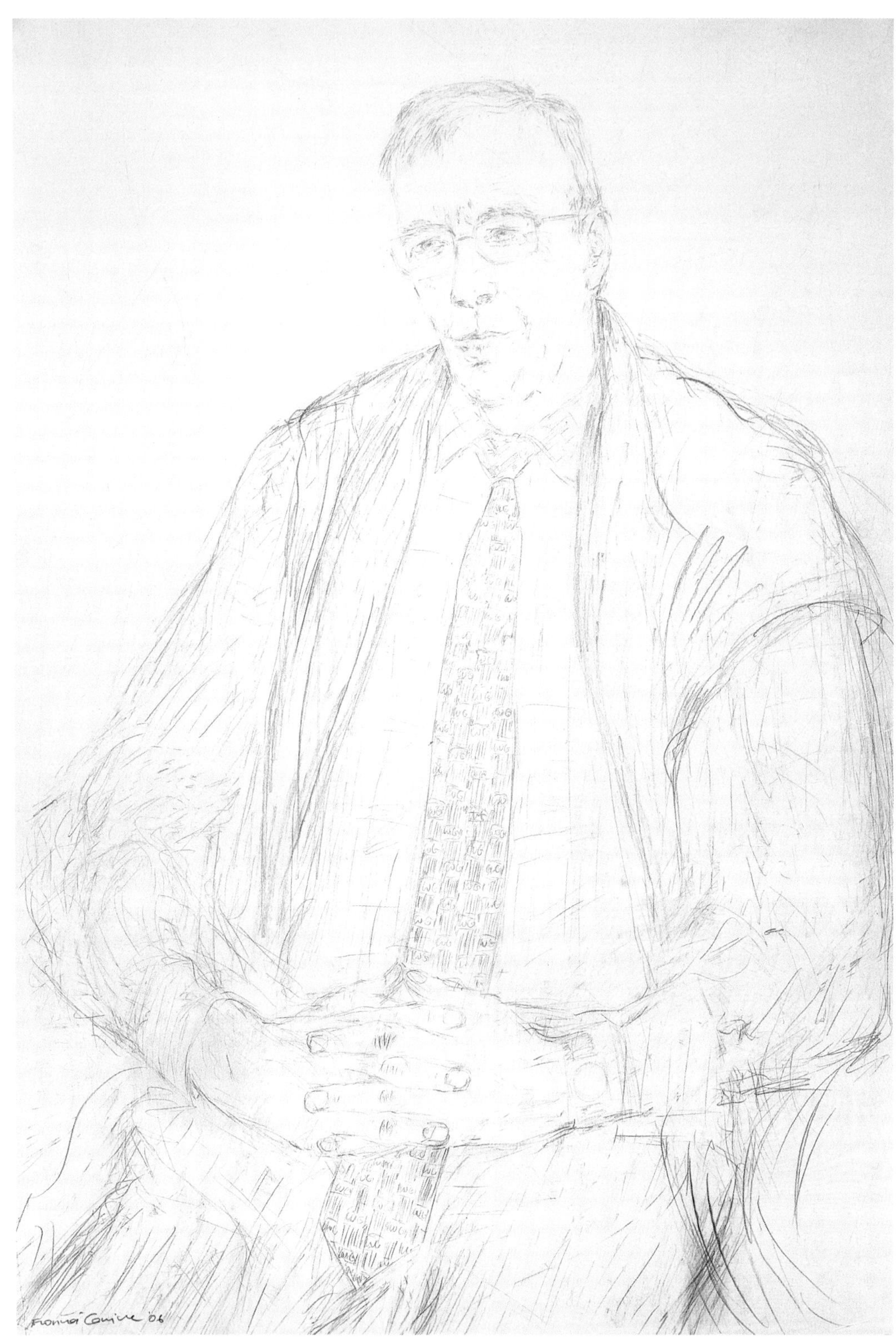

Sir Ian Wood, Chairman and Managing Director, John Wood Group PLC, 2006
Drawn in Aberdeen · pencil on paper, 83.5 x 59.9

would not believe in it. It would look artificial. Instead we have pictures that record the individuals in ways that are strikingly distinct, but also which capture something of the artist's own experience in what has been a kind of voyage of discovery. What from the outside may look like a business of steel structures like space stations and labyrinths of hydra-headed pipes is in fact an extraordinarily close community of very diverse individuals. It is with justifiable pride that she records herself in a painting, outside on the deck of Alwyn North with those intricate pipes behind her, wearing orange overalls and a green hard hat. In this picture the artist takes her place in the community.

Professor Alex Kemp [p.30], who stands out in this company in his dark suit and tie, takes his place here as one of the leading experts on the North Sea oil and gas industry. He knows it intimately at the human level as well as the statistical. He says it is like a village. Chris Christie [p.35] who has worked in the industry all her life calls it a family. People know each other and it is criss-crossed by relationships which are human as well as practical. There is a friendliness in the industry which surely springs from the natural solidarity of people working in dangerous circumstances; not all do, of course, but that experience remains at the heart of it. As in a village, too, there are individuals who stand out, not because of their position in any hierarchy, but simply for who they are and the impact they

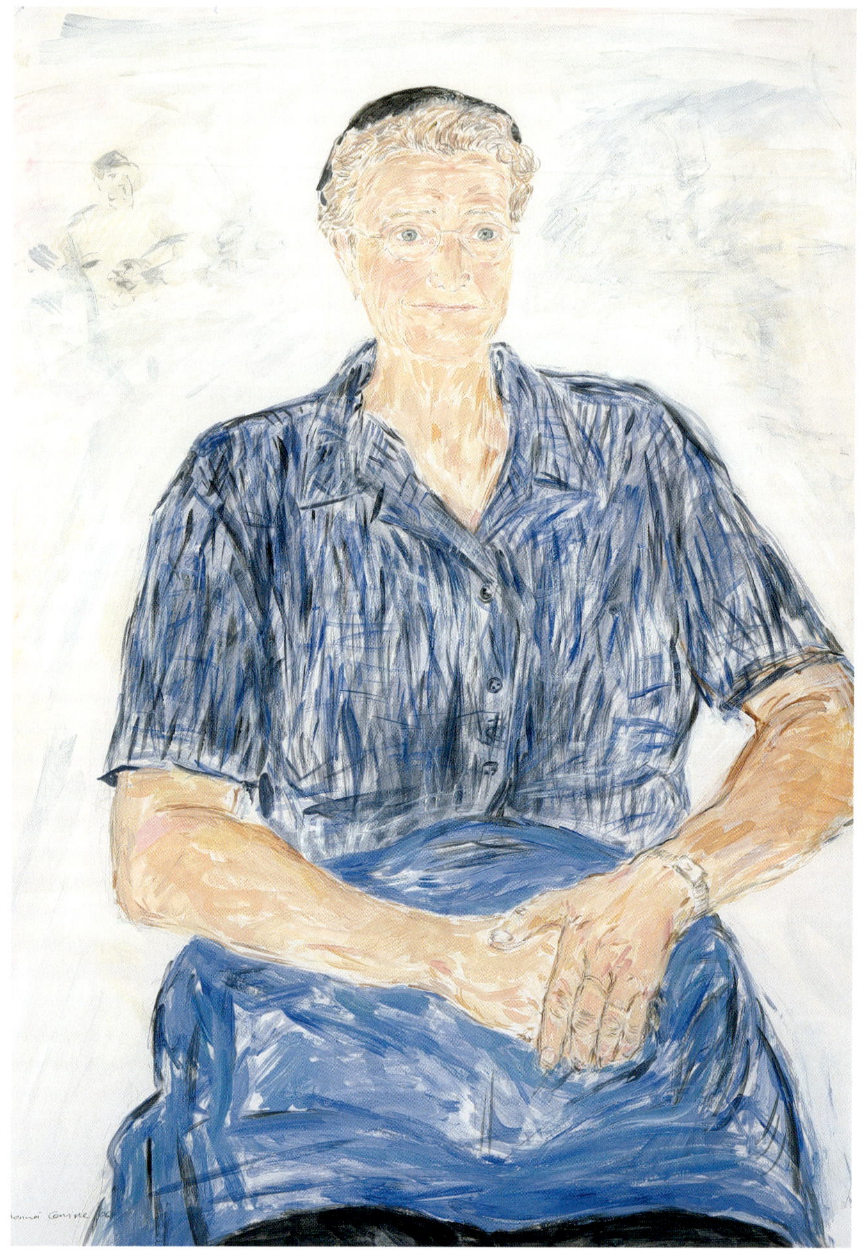

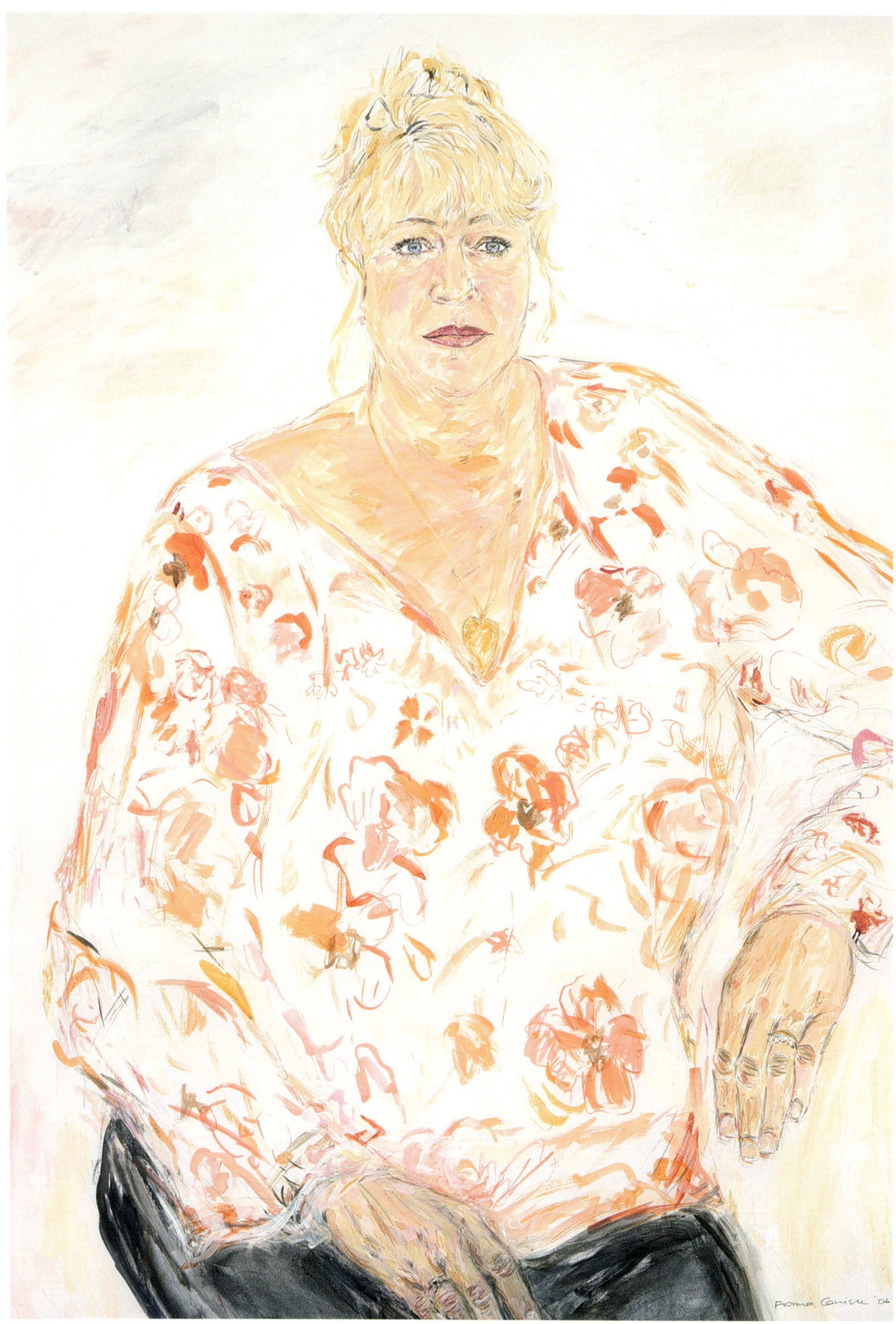

Jean Stephen, General Assistant / Coffee Lady, ESS Aberdeen, 2006
Painted in Aberdeen · acrylic on paper, 83.5 x 59.9

Chris Christie, Operational HR Advisor for Azerbaijan Business Unit, BP Group, 2006
Painted in Edinburgh · acrylic on paper, 83.5 x 59.9

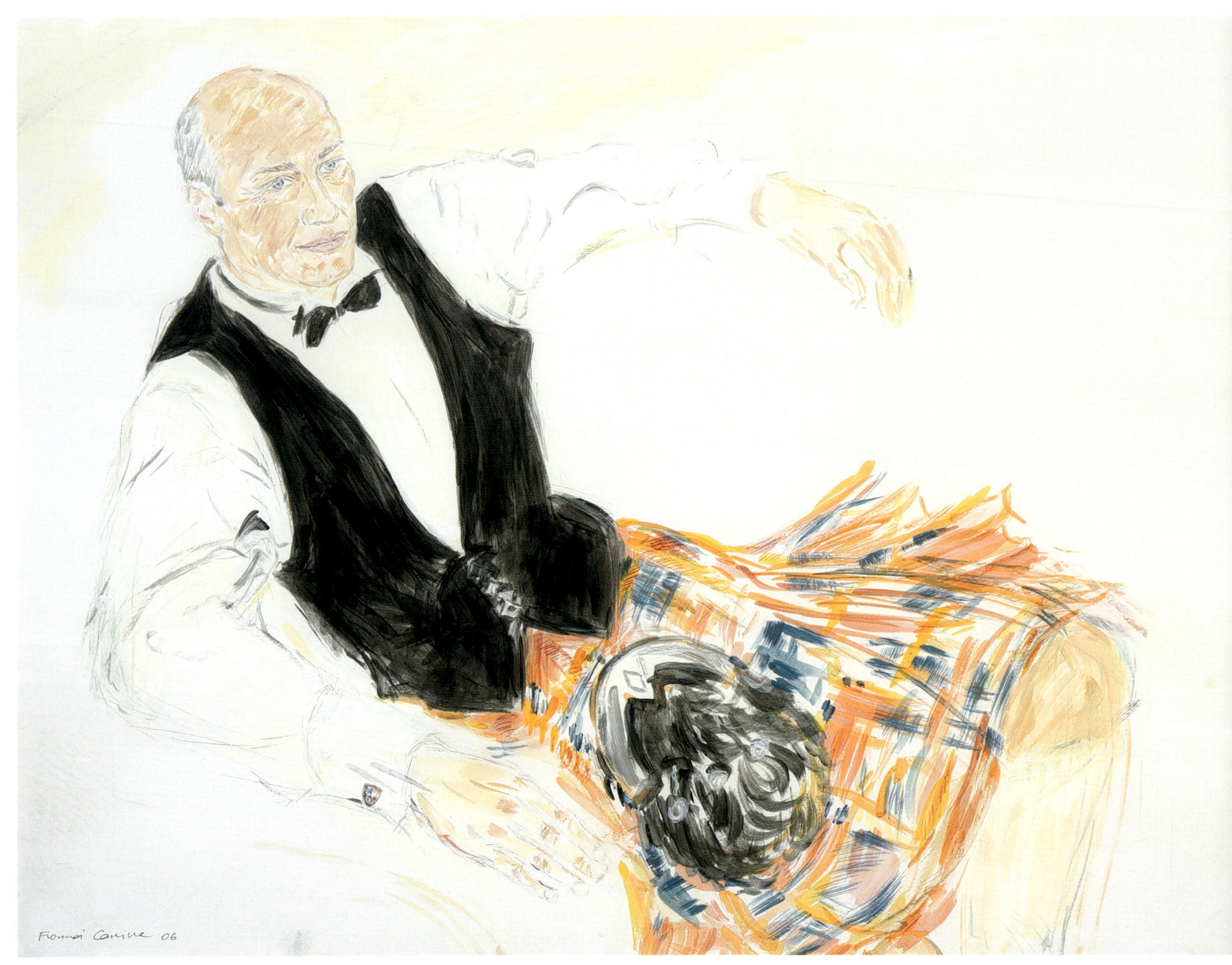

Andrew Hogg, Public Affairs & Corporate Communication Manager, Total, 2006
Painted in Aberdeen and Edinburgh
Acrylic and watercolour on paper, 59.9 x 83.5

have made in the community. Chris herself is one of these for instance. The mother of the North Sea she is called, and now, she told me with justified pride, she is known as the mother of the Caspian too. Her portrait captures the warmth and generosity that has earned her that sobriquet. Her story is typical of many of those here. She wanted to be a nurse, began with a humble job in BP, moved into Human Resources, gradually moved up within the company until with the oil price crash in 1998 she went independent. Now she handles recruitment and training for the new oil fields in the Caspian and commutes to Baku. Robert Youngman (Rab the Rigger), and David McKeon (the Silver Fox), are equally conspicuous characters in the community. Rab began life as a boy seaman in the merchant navy and sailed from Lerwick to Bangkok at the age of sixteen. Indeed as the artist herself says, everyone has a story and she has heard them too. Sitting for her seems to bring out confessions, or at least life stories, she says.

One way in which the sitters were chosen was by a ballot taken around the industry. Who were the people who counted and should be recorded? To his own surprise, but perhaps nobody else's, Lord Cullen came near the top of the poll. He is a modest man and saw the report he undertook following the Piper Alpha disaster in 1988 as just a job he had to do. But the contribution his report has made to safety in the industry has been recognised worldwide. Austin Hand [p.43] was another who came high in the ballot. He had been director of the Goldeneye development for Shell UK, a technologically ambitious project with a long undersea pipeline bringing the gas ashore to St Fergus. The St Fergus terminal itself reflects the changes in the industry, as it is a site shared by several major oil companies.

But other things entered into it too. There were people whom Fionna met and who helped her like Neil Poole [p.18], for instance. Called the Jolly Green Giant for his green medic's uniform, he was recorded because he lent her his first-aid room as a studio on Elgin-Franklin.

Thus the sitters range from Michel Contie who presides over Total from above like a hawk – and the artist has captured something of the condor in his fierce gaze – to Jean Stephen [p.34] in the canteen, who knows the industry almost as well as he does though from a very different perspective. No matter how long you may have been away, or how far you have travelled in the industry's worldwide network, she will still remember how you take your coffee. The Reverend Angus Smith also has personal connections right across the industry. He was a great help in making contacts for the artist and suggesting people who could stand as its representatives.

Indeed the strength of this collection is how extremes are linked. The common ground the sitters share is more important than any hierarchy to which they might belong. And that is something we read in the paintings. It is the artist who has articulated it so clearly.

If men like the Silver Fox or Rab the Rigger represent the kind of macho figures doing tough physical jobs who in the popular imagination might be associated with the oil industry, this collection as a whole also dispels the simplification of that image. Chris Christie, for instance, in her floral top, is in striking feminine counterpoint to such macho images and Fionna Carlisle's portraits record how women have begun to make their way in the industry, not only onshore, but offshore too. In the Norwegian sector this has been the norm since the beginning, but the Scottish sector was slower to open up to women. Laure Veyradier has the top job of OIM, but when the artist was with her on Elgin-Franklin, they were the only two women on the platform.

Nevertheless, women are there now in some numbers. Dr Alison Carroll of Abermed [p.40] was one of the first woman doctors to work offshore, for instance. Anne-Maree Beedie of ESS [p.42], who works in catering offshore is one of the youngest people here. Nicola Park [pp.26-7] from the St Fergus Gas Terminal is strikingly feminine, but she is also a fully qualified process supervisor dressed in orange overalls and with the tools of her trade strapped to her belt. She stands beautifully, the artist observed, and later learnt that she also plays in a pipe band. The administrator of St Fergus, is also a woman, Jennifer Wink [p.31], though keeping the balance of the sexes, the head of operations there, is a man, John Burns [p.24]. Alison Goligher [p.21] is, like Laure Veyradier, a woman who has risen

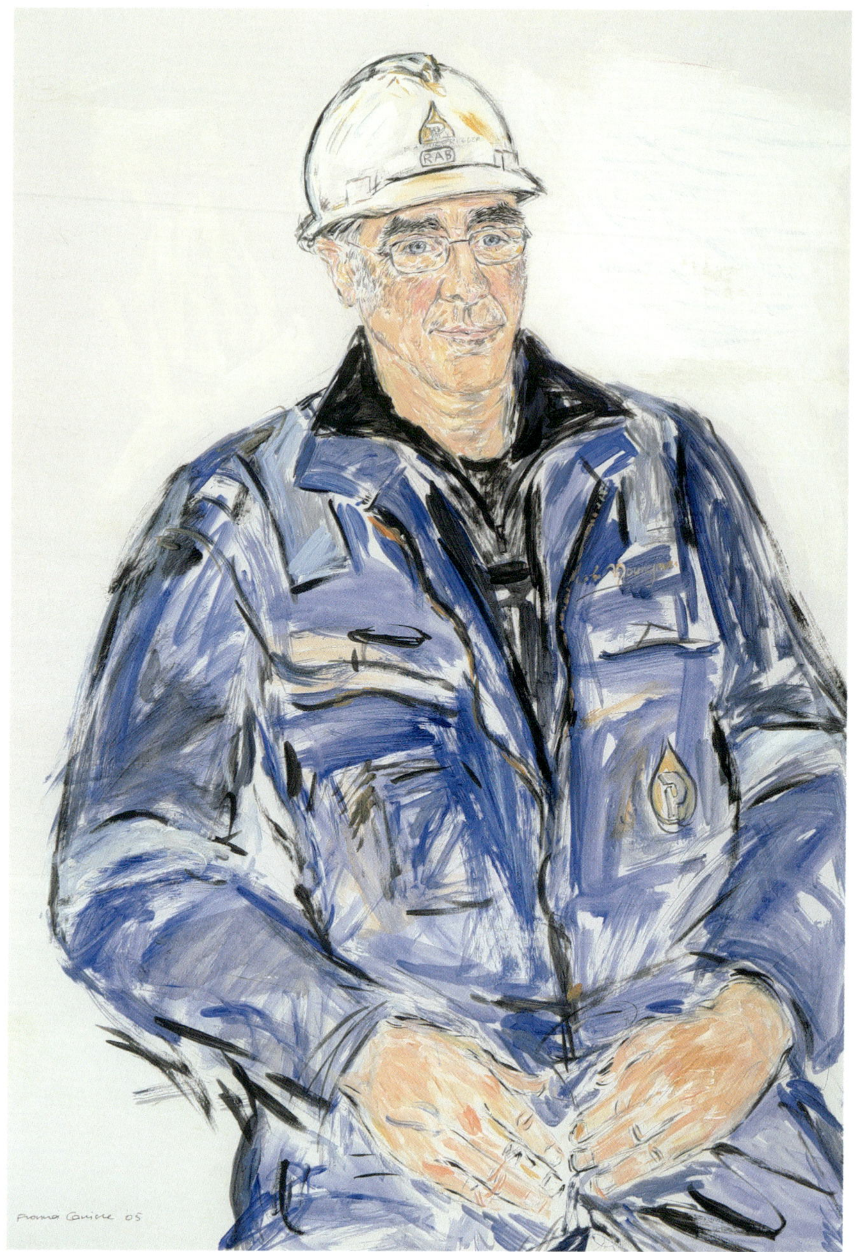

Robert Youngman, Rigger, Alwyn North, Petrofac Facilities Management, 2005
Painted on Alwyn North · acrylic on paper, 83.5 x 59.9

David McKeon, Survival Instructor, Rubicon Response Ltd, 2006
Painted in Aberdeen · acrylic on paper, 83.5 x 59.9

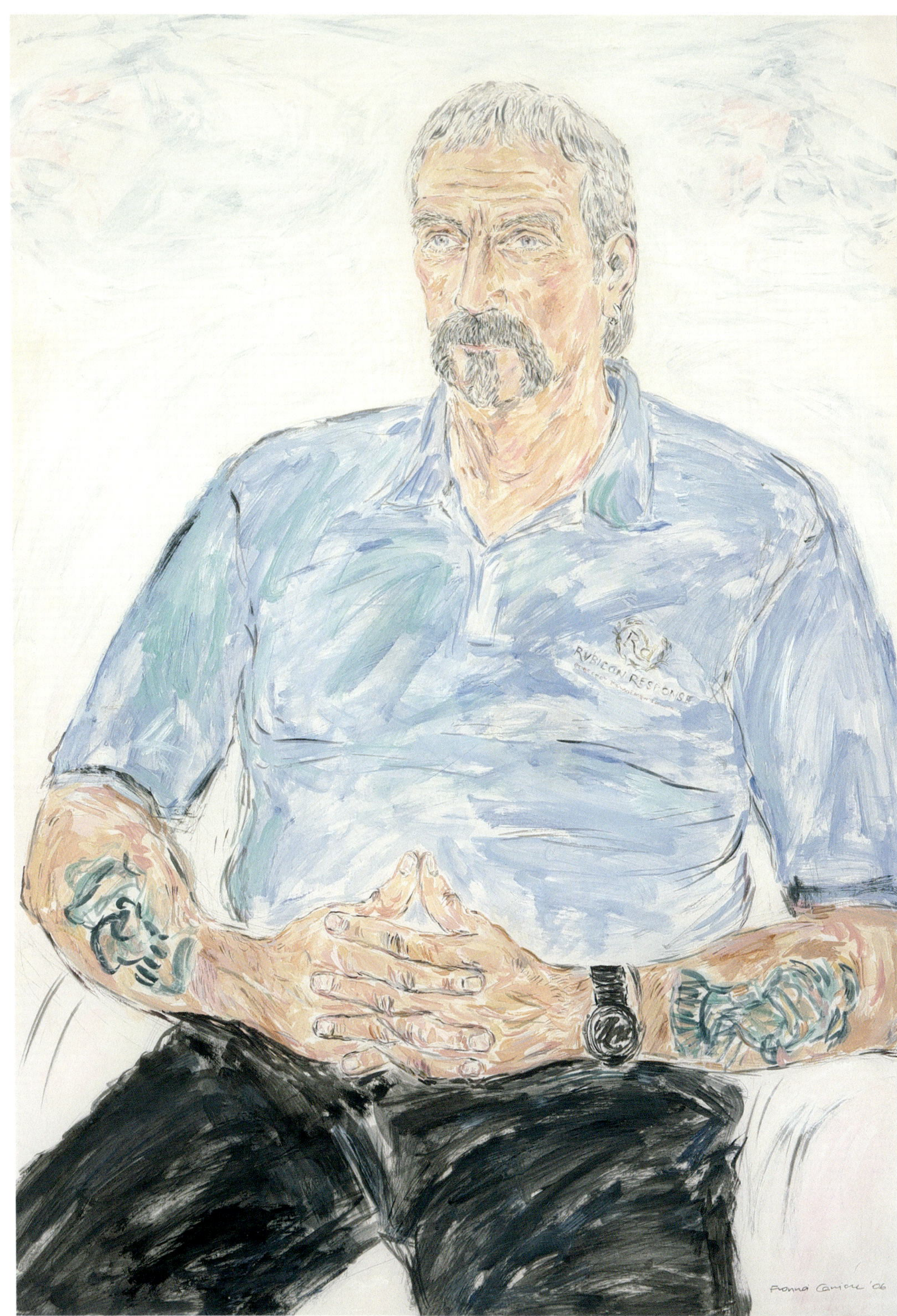

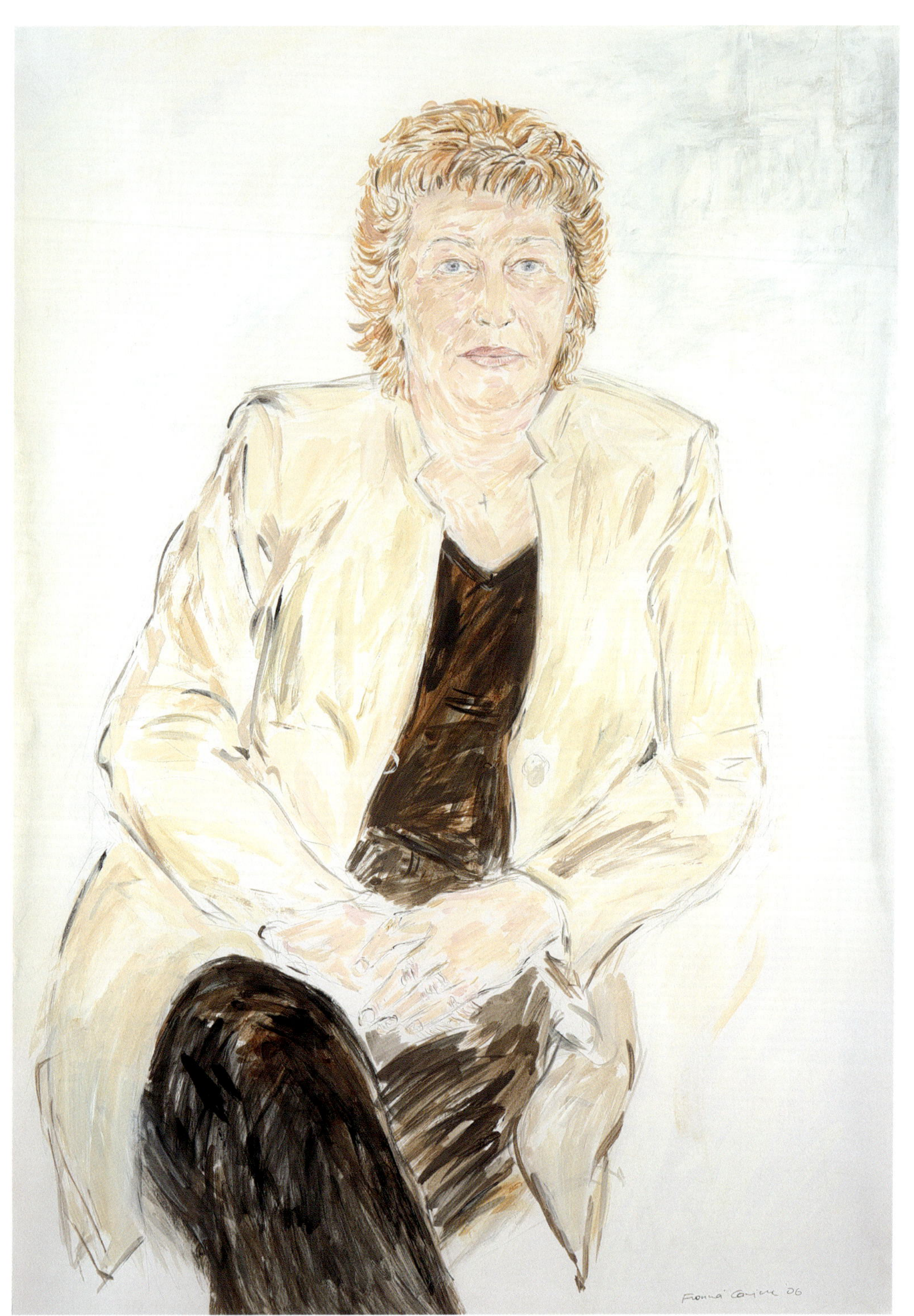

Dr Alison Carroll, Senior Medical Advisor, Abermed Ltd, 2006

Painted in Aberdeen · acrylic on paper, 83.5 x 59.9

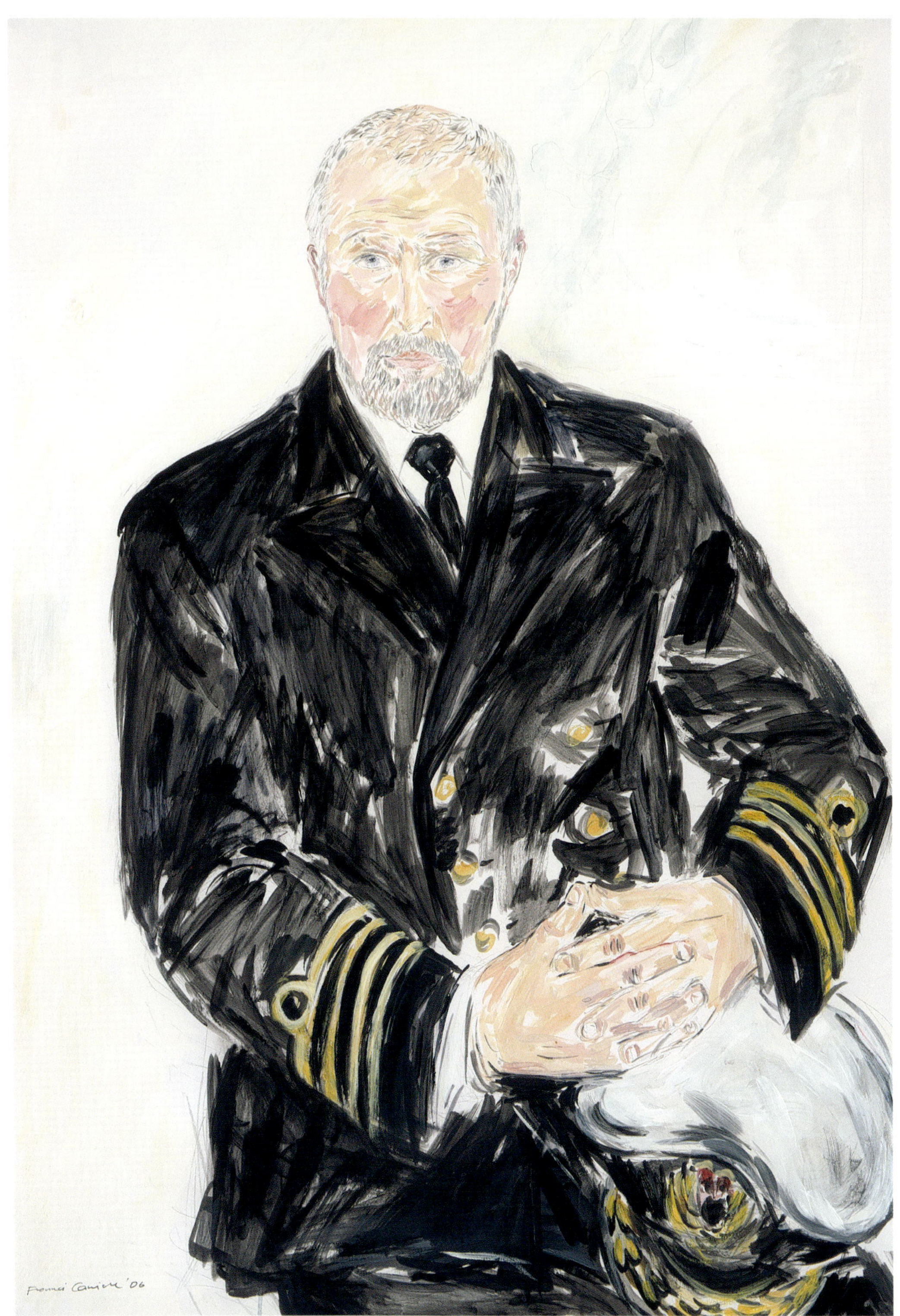

Captain Archer T. L. Kemp, Harbourmaster, Lerwick, Shetland, 2006

Painted in Lerwick, Shetland

Acrylic on paper, 83.5 x 59.9

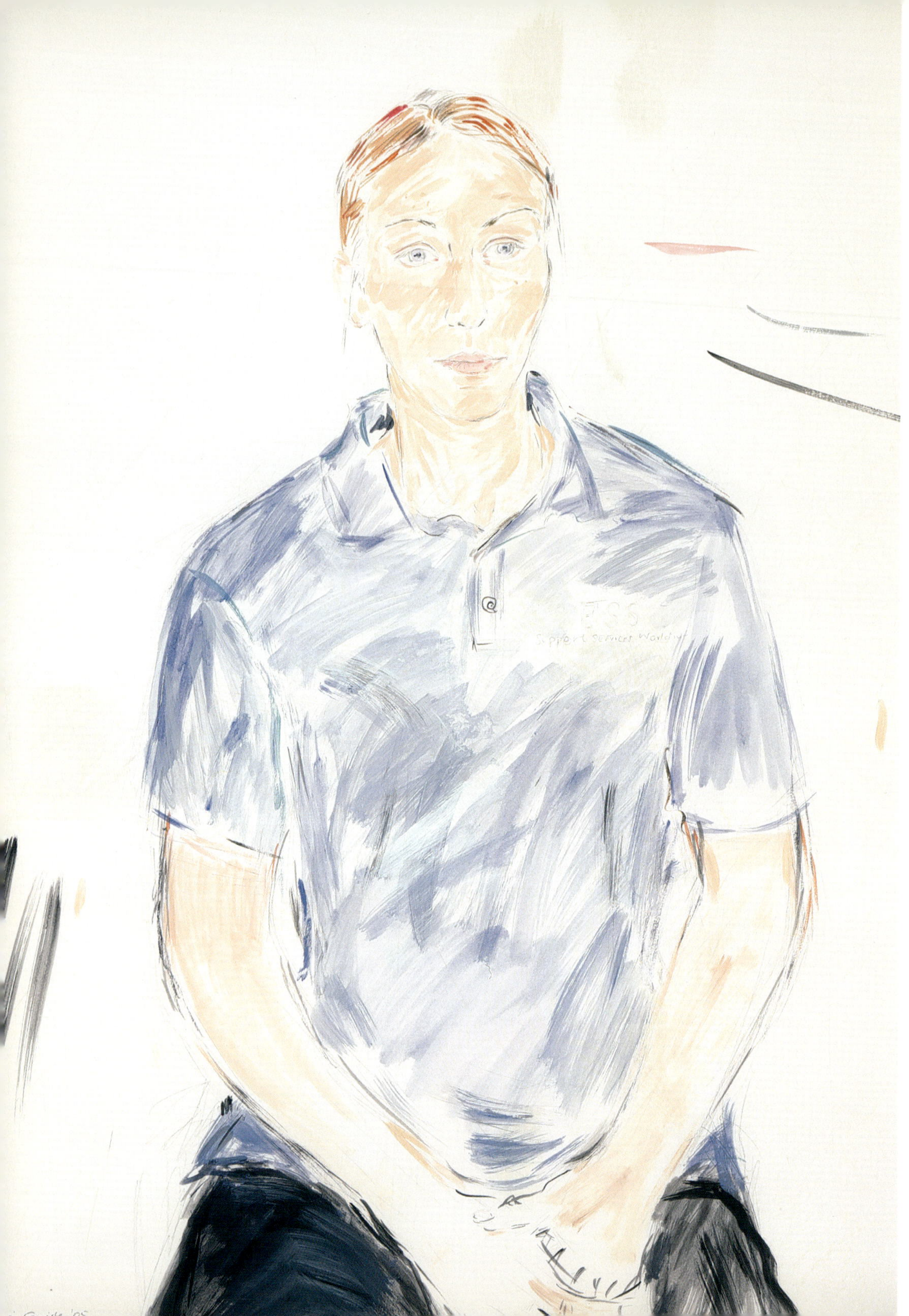

Anne-Maree Beedie, Stewardess, Elgin-Franklin, ESS Aberdeen, 2005
Painted on Elgin-Franklin · acrylic on paper, 83.5 x 59.9

Austin Hand, General Manager Engineering and Projects, Shell, 2006
Painted in Aberdeen · acrylic on paper, 83.5 x 59.9

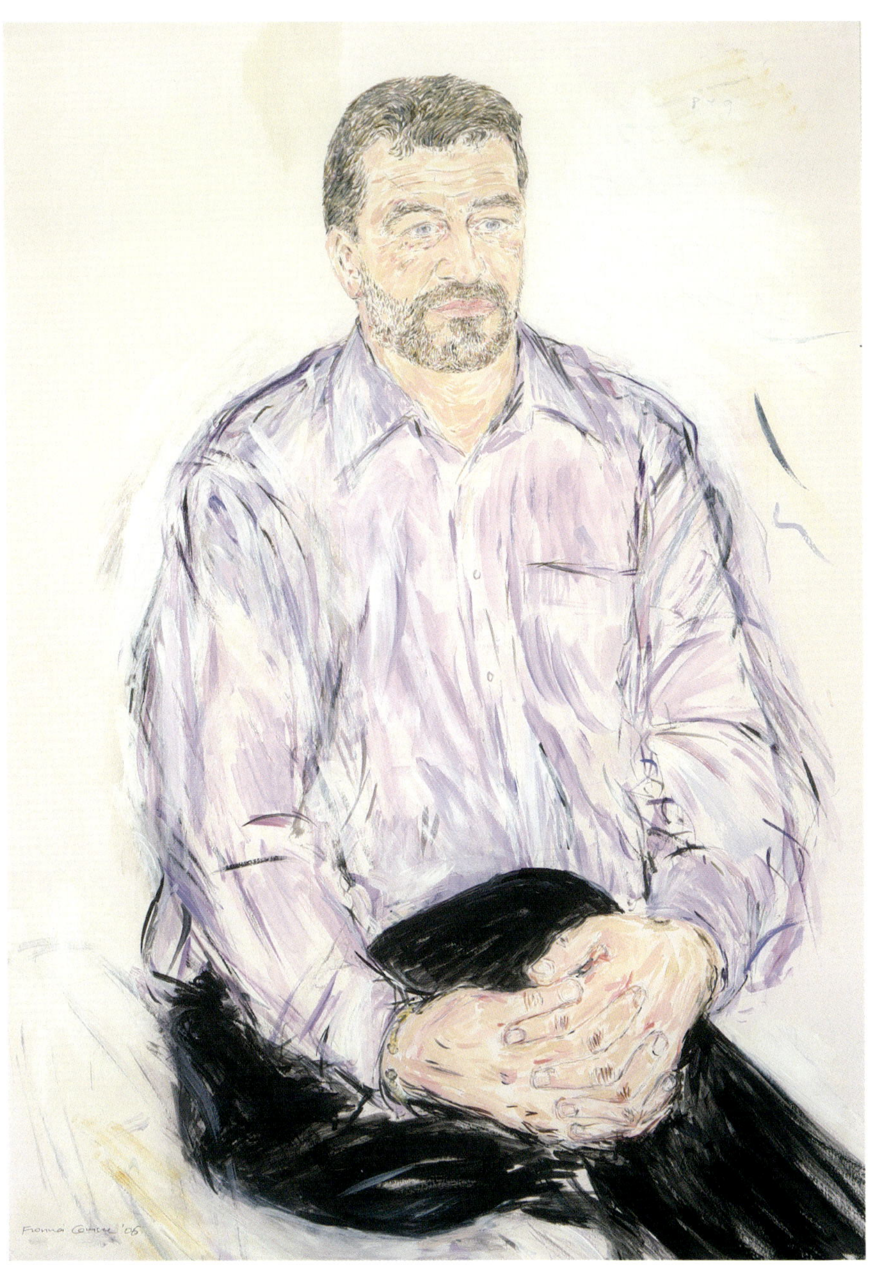

high in the business. She is painted in the blue overalls of Schlumberger, the global service company of which she was a UK vice-president. On her lap is a white helmet, a symbol of the priority the modern oil and gas industry places on safety.

In a curious way the whole remarkable story of North Sea oil has passed us by, hitherto. Where are the songs and tall tales that an adventure of this kind would once have generated? It has had its tragedies, certainly – the oil industry as a whole is still marked by the terrible disaster of Piper Alpha. These have touched the wider public too; but up till now the story of North Sea oil has not really had the imaginative impact it deserves. Is the reason for this as Lord Cullen suggested to me simply that it is over the horizon and out of sight? Oil and gas have had an enormous economic impact certainly. Centred on Aberdeen, the industry is the most wealth-creating of all production and manufacturing sectors in the UK. In 2006, total employment dependent on it will be 380,000. (UKCS Economic Estimates) But that colossal economic impact is not immediately obvious. It is not marked by monumental public buildings, nor by any of the traditional visible signs of economic success. There has apparently not even been new infrastructure. Oil and gas pipelines are underground and invisible. Now finally this exhibition acknowledges its achievement, records it for posterity and above all the artist's remarkable portraits give it a memorable human face.

Biographies of the Sitters

ANNE-MAREE BEEDIE

Born Fraserburgh, 1980 · Stewardess, Elgin-Franklin, ESS Aberdeen

Anne-Maree is employed through ESS. Her duties include cleaning the accommodation on the rig and working in the galley. She has been off-shore for six years, working a two-on-two-off rota.

JOHN BEY

Born Huntly, Aberdeenshire, 1967 · Control Room Operator, Alwyn North, TOTAL E&P UK PLC

Since 1988, John has worked as an industrial cleaner carrying out low specific activity radiation decontamination of oil separator vessels. In 1995 he joined Expro North Sea Ltd as a trainee wireline operator, and by 1999 was wireline supervisor on Alwyn North. He joined Total in 2005.

JOHN BURNS

Born Aberdeen, 1950 · Head of Operations, St Fergus Gas Terminal, TOTAL E&P UK PLC

John joined Total Oil Marine in 1976, becoming a process operator. In 1980 he was seconded to Norway to work on the Ekofisk Project to obtain commissioning experience for compressors. In 1981 he transferred offshore and was duty supervisor on the night of the Piper Alpha disaster. He became plant superintendent of St Fergus in 1994. In 1997 he became production superintendent on Alwyn North.

DR ALISON CARROLL

Born Aberdeen, 1954 · Senior Medical Advisor, Abermed Ltd

Alison qualified in medicine in Aberdeen in 1978 and studied psychiatry in Aberdeen, Glasgow and Edinburgh. She has worked in the oil and gas industry for fifteen years, based in the North Sea, Africa and the former Soviet Union. She is now the medical director of Abermed, a private occupational health company founded in the 1980s to service the oil and gas industry.

CHRIS CHRISTIE

Born Banffshire, 1958 · Operational HR Advisor for Azerbaijan Business Unit, BP Group

Chris has worked with BP for twenty-eight years. Thirteen years were spent offshore in the North Sea working in a logistics personnel and training role on the Magnus, ETAP, and Bruce platforms. She also spent eleven years onshore with BP based in Aberdeen. She is now based in London where she handles recruitment for expatriates in the projects and operations teams.

MICHEL CONTIE, DBA

Born France, 1948 · Senior Vice-President Northern Europe & UK Country Representative, TOTAL

Michel is a former managing director of TOTAL E&P UK PLC. He is a former vice-president of the United Kingdom Offshore Operators' Association (UKOOA) and a member of PILOT, the UK government / oil industry organisation. His honours include Officer of the Ordre National de Mérite, awarded by the French government and doctorate of business administration from the Robert Gordon University, Aberdeen.

LORD (WILLIAM DOUGLAS) CULLEN OF WHITEKIRK

Born Edinburgh, 1935

Lord Cullen was called to the Scottish Bar in 1960. He was appointed Advocate – Depute in 1977 and Lord Justice Clerk in 1997, and Senator of the College of Justice in 1986. From 1988 to 1990 Lord Cullen was chairman of the inquiry into the Piper Alpha disaster. The Cullen Report that came from this inquiry has resulted in the provision of safer working practices throughout the oil industry.

BILL EDGAR, CBE

Born Blantyre, 1938 · Chairman of Subsea UK, President of The Institution of Mechanical Engineers, 2004–5

Bill was managing director of Seaforth Engineering in 1973-6 and subsequently engineering director of Seaforth Maritime Group, Aberdeen. He has also served as director of Vickers Marine and Offshore Division, Edinburgh and chief executive of the National Engineering Laboratory, East Kilbride. From 1995–2004 he was group director of John Wood Group PLC, Aberdeen.

ALISON GOLIGHER

Born Belfast, Northern Ireland, 1965 · Vice-President, Corporate Support, Shell E&P Europe

Alison joined Schlumberger Oilfield Services in 1988 as a field engineer in Brunei before postings to the Far East, USA, Norway and France. In 2001 she became managing director with responsibility for all business segments of Oilfield Services in the UK, Ireland and Faroes. Awards include an honorary degree (LLD) from Dundee University for services to the oil and gas industry and an OBE (2005).

AUSTIN HAND

Born Stockton-on Tees, 1949 · General Manager Engineering and Projects, Shell UK Ltd

Austin is a mechanical engineer who joined Shell in 1978. He worked on Inde, Dunlin and Cormorant Alpha Platforms before becoming project manager for Kingfisher, Curlew and Triton. He was venture manager for the Goldeneye development in the outer Moray Firth. Still based in Aberdeen, his team is working for projects in Gabon, Nigeria, Qatar, Iran, Russia, and Europe.

ANDREW HOGG

Born Wexford, Ireland, 1960 · Public Affairs & Corporate Communication Manager, TOTAL E&P UK PLC

After degrees in Dublin, Toronto and Aberdeen, Andrew worked for fourteen years with BP as a sedimentologist and development geologist. He was the recipient of a BP Exploration Award for Technical Achievement for his work on the Wytch Farm Extended Reach Development Project. Following a period in business development in Kuwait he moved into public affairs, working on UK-Norway co-operation on oil and gas. He has been in his current post with Total since 2003.

PROFESSOR ALEX KEMP

Born Drumoak, Aberdeenshire · Professor of Petroleum Economics, University of Aberdeen

Alex was an economist for Shell before becoming an academic researching petroleum economics with special reference to the North Sea. He has published over 200 papers and books in this field and has advised many governments, oil companies, and the World Bank on these matters. He is writing the *Official History of North Sea Oil and Gas*. In 2006 Professor Kemp was awarded the OBE for services to the oil and gas industries.

CAPTAIN ARCHER T.L. KEMP

Born Orkney, 1948 · Harbourmaster, Lerwick, Shetland

Archer began his career in the Merchant Navy, qualifying as master mariner in 1973. After an international sea-going career, he moved to the North Sea in 1976 as master of an anchor-handling tug. He joined Atlantic Drilling in 1977 and became an offshore installation manager in 1980, serving in this capacity until coming ashore to join Lerwick Port Authority in 1993. He has been harbourmaster since 1987.

COLIN KING

Born Orkney, 1960 · Offshore Installation Manager (OIM), Alwyn North, TOTAL E&P UK PLC

From 1977–87 Colin was instrument technician on the Flotta Oil Terminal in Orkney and Dounreay before moving offshore in 1987. In 1994 he became OIM and in 1997, commissioning manager for Total's Elgin-Franklin HP/HT (high pressure / high temperature) development in the central North Sea, building three platforms, at Nigg, Inverness-shire and on Teesside. In 2001, he became OIM on Elgin-Franklin before transferring to Alwyn North in 2004.

JOSEPH LAHBIB

Born Montaubon, France, 1941 · Catering Facilites Manager, Alwyn North, TOTAL E&P UK PLC

Joseph worked as a chef in 5-star hotels including the Hotel de Paris, Monte Carlo and Gleneagles Hotel in Scotland before graduating to facilities management in the oil industry. He has worked for twenty-five years on Total operated platforms.

DAVID McKEON

Born London, 1949 · Survival Instructor, Rubicon Response Ltd

David has been a survival and helicopter underwater escape training instructor for twenty-two years. He presents helicopter safety videos before all offshore oil industry flights. He provides advice and instruction for both emergency response team members, onshore and offshore installation managers and control room team members.

NICOLA PARK

Born Aberdeen, 1978 · Control Room Operator, St Fergus Gas Terminal, AkerKvaerner Offshore Partner Ltd

After studying electrical engineering at Jewel & Esk Valley College and Leith Nautical College, Nicola became an apprentice electrical technician at Total's St Fergus Gas Terminal in 1995. As control room operator she works a shift rota which involves night and day shifts. She is also part of the emergency response team.

NEIL POOLE

Born Stoke on Trent, 1956 · Offshore Medic, Elgin-Franklin, Abermed Ltd

Neil is an ex-army combat medical technician, HSE first aid instructor and examiner. After leaving the army in 1992, he went offshore, working for RGIT, Abermed and Capita as an offshore medic. Mainly based in the North Sea, he has occasionally made trips to Iran and Moscow to work as a medic. He has lived in Spain for the last six years.

ALEX SALMOND

Born Linlithgow, 1954 · Leader of the Scottish National Party, Member of Parliament for Banff and Buchan, and Oil Economist

In 1980, Alex joined the Royal Bank of Scotland as an oil economist. He was first elected as Member of Parliament in 1987 and became leader of the SNP in 1990. He served in the Scottish Parliament until 2001, but remains an MP at Westminster. Alex has promoted the development of carbon capture and renewable energy producers, and argued for Scotland to receive revenues from North Sea oil.

SYED MAQSOOD SHER

Born Karachi, Pakistan, 1951 · Group Operations Manager and Executive Vice-President, Orient Petroleum Company

Maqsood has worked for Conoco and Total in the Middle East, France, Argentina, Yemen and the UK. He was production superintendent for Alwyn North during 1993–5 and as UK operated assets operations manager in 2001. He played a key role in making Elgin-Franklin the best performing asset in the North Sea.

REVEREND ANGUS SMITH

Born Keose Glebe, Isle of Lewis, 1936 · Former Oil and Gas Industry Chaplain (1991–2006)

Reverend Smith studied in Glasgow and Aberdeen before becoming ordained a Church of Scotland minister in 1965. He served both as a parish minister and army chaplain, and his postings included Aberdeen, London, Northern Ireland and the South Atlantic. In 1991, he became chaplain to the oil industry, providing pastoral ministry for both offshore and onshore workers.

JEAN STEPHEN

Born Dunecht, 1940 · General Assistant / Coffee Lady, ESS Aberdeen

Jean has worked for ESS based at TOTAL E&P UK's Altens office as the 'coffee lady' for twenty-nine years. Before taking up this position, Jean spent her time bringing up her four children.

LAURE VEYRADIER

Born France, 1969 · Offshore Installations Manager (OIM), Elgin-Franklin, TOTAL E&P UK PLC

Laure studied chemical engineering in Lyon and Madrid. She has worked for fourteen years in the oil industry in operations of production, in Angola, Congo, Arab Emirates and Scotland. She worked with Elf from 1992 until the merger between Total and Elf in 2000. She is now based on Elgin-Franklin, spending one week in five in Total's office in Aberdeen.

JENNIFER WINK

Born Peterhead, 1964 · Administration Supervisor, St Fergus Gas Terminal, TOTAL E&P UK PLC

Jennifer gained an HNC in accounting before becoming administration supervisor at St Fergus Gas Terminal. She manages the onsite ESS facilities management contract, all office services and maintenance, and local corporate committees dealing with issues of waste management, security and information technology.

SIR IAN WOOD, CBE

Born Aberdeen, 1942 · Chairman and Managing Director, John Wood Group PLC

Sir Ian joined the family business, John Wood & Son in 1964. This has now evolved into two independent Scottish business groups: John Wood Group PLC, providing engineering and high technology services and products to offshore oil and gas, power generation and general industrial markets worldwide, and J.W. Holdings Ltd, one of the largest fishing companies in Scotland. Sir Ian was awarded CBE in 1982.

ROBERT YOUNGMAN

Born, Lerwick, Shetland Isles, 1945 · Rigger, Petrofac Facilities Management

After attending Leith Nautical College, Robert (Rab) joined the Merchant Navy at the age of fifteen. He spent almost twenty years deep sea trawling out of Aberdeen. He has worked as a rigger on many offshore installations and for many companies and has been maintenance rigger on the Alwyn North for seventeen years.

Fionna Carlisle

Born Wick, Caithness, Scotland

EDUCATION AND AWARDS

1972–6 Edinburgh College of Art
1976–7 Andrew Grant Postgraduate Scholarship, Edinburgh College of Art
1979 Awarded Meyer Oppenheim Prize, Royal Scottish Academy
1982 Scottish Arts Council Bursary, used for travel to China
1999–2003 Artist in Residence, Caledonian Brewery, Edinburgh
2005 Icon of Scotland, Visual Arts, New York

PATRON

Spinal Injuries Scotland

SOLO EXHIBITIONS

1978–81 369 Gallery, Edinburgh
1981 The Fine Art Society, Glasgow; Lothian Region Travelling Exhibition
1982 369 Gallery, Edinburgh
1984 The Traverse Theatre, Edinburgh
1986 369 Gallery, Edinburgh
1988 The Barbican Centre, London
1990 Mayfair Fine Art, London
1991 Calart, Geneva
1992 369 Gallery, London
1995/7 The Scottish Gallery, Edinburgh
1998 *Portraits on Paper*, Scottish Arts Club, Edinburgh
2000 *Crete & Caithness*, Northlands Festival, St Fergus Gallery, Wick and Ackergill Tower
2001 Archeus Fine Art, London

SELECTED GROUP EXHIBITIONS

1974/6 Saltire Gallery, Edinburgh
1977 New 57 Group Show, Edinburgh
1978 Royal Scottish Academy
1978–80 Royal Scottish Society of Painters in Watercolour, Edinburgh
1980 The Fruitmarket Gallery, Edinburgh; Browse & Darby, London
1981 The Fine Art Society, Edinburgh, Glasgow and London; *Edinburgh Behind the Facade*, Scottish Arts Council Travelling Exhibition; *Scottish Painting*, Watts Gallery, Phoenix, Arizona; Royal Scottish Society of Painters in Watercolour, Edinburgh
1982 *Five Women Artists*, Traverse Theatre, Edinburgh; Watts Gallery, Phoenix, Arizona; The Fine Art Society, Edinburgh, Glasgow and London
1983 *Best of 369*, University of St Andrews; *Scottish Contemporary Art*, Clare Hall, Cambridge; *Scottish Expressionism*, 369 Gallery, Edinburgh; *Peintres Contemporains Ecossais*, Galerie Peinture Fraiche, Paris; *The Scottish Expression: 1983*, Freidus/Ordover Gallery, New York; *New Directions British Art*, Puck Building, New York
1983–9 Chicago International Art Exposition
1984 International Contemporary Arts Fair, London; *Scottish Expressionism*, Warwick Arts Trust, London and 369 Gallery; *Demarcations*, Edinburgh College of Art; Dart Gallery, Chicago; *Portraits on Paper*, Scottish Arts Council Touring Exhibition
1985 *Contemporary Scottish Landscape*, Edinburgh City Arts Centre; *Scottish Painting*. Linda Durham Gallery, Santa Fe, New Mexico
1986 Le Cadre Gallery, Hong Kong; Los Angeles Contemporary Art Fair
1987–8 *Contemporary Scottish Landscape*, Highland Region Tour
1988 *Scottish Expressionism*, 369 Gallery
1989 *Coldhouse Soo*, Soo Terminal Building, Chicago; *Contemporary Scottish Painting*, The Palace of Youth, Moscow; *Scottish Expressionism*, 369 Gallery
1989–90 *Scottish Art since 1900*, Scottish National Gallery of Modern Art, Edinburgh and Barbican Gallery, London
1990 *Scottish Expressionism*, 369 Gallery
1991 *Edinburgh/Moscow*, The Georgian Cultural Centre, Moscow; Moscow International Art Fair
1992–3 *In Other Lands*, Highland Council, 369 Gallery, Edinburgh
1994 *Students Past and Present*, Heriot Watt University, Edinburgh College of Art; *The Colourist Legacy*, Edinburgh City Arts Centre
1995 *The Beltane Spirit*, Wick, Thurso, Kingussie and London, Highland Council Touring Exhibition
1996–2000 *Art 96*, Business Design Centre, London, with The Scottish Gallery, Edinburgh
1998 *Provost's Prize Exhibition*, Gallery of Modern Art, Glasgow
2000 *Expressions Scottish Art 1976–89*, Aberdeen Art Gallery, McManus Galleries, Dundee Contemporary Arts, Dundee
2002 *Artists of Xania*, Crete, Greece; *Adapt*, Kelvingrove Art Gallery, Glasgow; *Summer Show*, Open Eye Gallery, Edinburgh
2003 *Private Showing*, *Portrait of Sylvia Stevenson*, Tate Britain and Dean Gallery, Edinburgh
2004 *Modern Women*, Scottish National Portrait Gallery, Edinburgh
2005 *Offshore Europe Exposition*, Total E&P UK PLC, Aberdeen; *Scotsman Portraits*, Scottish National Portrait Gallery, Edinburgh
2006 Channel 4 Political Awards, London; *Thoroughly Modern Women*, Scottish National Portrait Gallery, Edinburgh; *Art in the Workplace*, Glasgow

COLLECTIONS

Scottish National Gallery of Modern Art; Scottish National Portrait Gallery; Scottish Arts Council Contemporary Arts Society; Dundee Art Gallery Edinburgh City Arts Centre; Glasgow Museums; Highland Regional Council; McLean Arts Gallery & Museum, Greenock; Motherwell District Council; Chelmsford Arts Gallery; Leeds Education Authority; 3i; Coopers & Lybrand; De Beers; IBM; Netherland Bank; Conoco Philips Petroleum; Robert Fleming Holdings Ltd; Stirling University; House of Commons Collection and private collections in Britain, Europe, and North and South America.

THE AUTHORS

PROFESSOR DUNCAN MACMILLAN
MA PhD HON.LLD FRSA FRSE HRSA
is an art historian, art critic and former gallery director and is Professor Emeritus in the University of Edinburgh. His book *Scottish Art 1460–1990* was Scottish Book of the Year when first published. He is also author of many other books, catalogues and articles and is art critic for *The Scotsman*.

DR BILL MACKIE MA PhD
is an historian and writer and former television producer and editor. He has written two books on the North Sea oil and gas industry, *The Oilmen: North Sea Tigers* on the offshore sector and a sequel, *The Klondykers: The Oilmen Onshore*.

Published by the Trustees of the National Galleries of Scotland to accompany the exhibition *Energy: North Sea Portraits* held at the Scottish National Portrait Gallery, Edinburgh from 25 October 2006 to 28 January 2007.

ISBN 1 903278 92 9 / 978 1903278 92 5

Paintings photographed by AIC Photographic Services
Other photographs © TOTAL E&P UK PLC
p. 11 © Rosa Steppanova
Typeset in Verdigris and Magma
Printed in Belgium by Die Keure

Cover: Colin King, Offshore Installation Manager (OIM), Alwyn North, 2004

Frontispiece: Fionna Carlisle and Colin King on Alwyn North

All dimensions are in centimetres height × width